D0120317

SEAN KINSELLA'S COOKBOOK

SEAN KINSELLA'S COOKBOOK

Culinary secrets of Ireland's
most famous chef

TOWN
HOUSE

Compiled by	Helen Quinn
Designed by	Wendy Dunbar
Photographer	Liam Blake
Drawings	Michael Craig
Text Editor	Siobhán Parkinson
Typesetting	Glynis Millar
Printing	Criterion Press, Dublin

© Copyright Seán Kinsella 1985
Published by
Town House, 2 Cambridge Villas, Rathmines, Dublin 6, Ireland
Distributed by Easons, Dublin
ISBN 0 948524 00 6

To my Mum and Dad,
my wife Audrey, her mother
and our two sons
Stephen and Andrew

AWARDS

— The United Dominion Trust Award 1981
— The Wedgwood Award for one of the top fifty restaurants in the world 1981
— The Gold Knife and Fork from Lyon 1977
— The Gold Ladle from Palm Beach 1980
— The Golden Spoon and Fork from Germany 1983
— The World's Famous International Restaurants Award 1973-1984
— The Chefs Anonymous Award from Los Angeles 1969
— The Gold Crown from *Sunset* Magazine California 1977
— Champagne Krug Reines Maison Recommandée Keug 1979

INTRODUCTION

Chefs are born, not made, they say. Perhaps they are, but in any case I was born in Cooraclare in County Clare. I got my first lesson in the commonsense approach to cookery when I watched my dad, who worked in the boiler room of the Richmond Hospital in Dublin, frying eggs to perfection – on a shovel. This just goes to show that you can manage with the minimum of equipment. I am told that I cooked my first breakfast standing on a butterbox at the age of seven when my parents were in bed sick.

My first job wasn't in the culinary art, but in Miller's Distillers in Thomas Street in Dublin. I was bottling whiskey during the summer holidays. In those days there was a trough with six brass pipes under the large vat, and when one of these pipes got an airlock I had to suck it free. The fumes made me very drowsy and a kindly foreman transferred me to the cordial warehouse. I was so relieved to be away from the whiskey fumes that I feel that must have been an important factor in my decision never to drink alcohol.

My first job as an apprentice chef was in Frascatti's in Suffolk Street, Dublin, and a year later I was interviewed by the managing director of the Gresham Hotel, Toddie O'Sullivan. When I told him I wanted to work in the Gresham because it was the best hotel in the world – which it was then – he said I could start next week. There I worked under the master chef Karl Uhlemann, author of the *Chef's Companion.* I obtained all my diplomas under his guidance. The day I left, Karl Uhlemann called me aside and, removing his tall chef's crown, said 'Son, I've been wearing this hat all my life and it's still the same size as it was the first time I wore it.' His message was clear – the day your head gets too big is the day you should leave the profession.

I am glad to say I am still learning. It is one of the joys of cooking that you can experiment to your heart's content and indulge your creativity. In fact I think people get too hung up on recipes, and my advice is don't be afraid to experiment – if you haven't got the ingredient listed substitute something else or leave it out altogether. Now that we have begun to rethink our use of salt, who misses it? And another thing – an artist never measures the amount of paint on his brush, so in using this book remember that the amounts given are just for guidance, to be adjusted as you cook.

After the Gresham I worked for the summer in the famous Jammet's restaurant, which stood in Nassau Street, where the Berni Inn is today, serving all French cuisine under the late Vincent Dowling. A wonderful period in the Commodore Hotel in Cork stirred my seagoing ambitions – in those days we were able to board the great passenger liners when they were docked in Cobh.

After some time I applied to the P & O Steam Navigation Company for a job on the SS *Oransay I,* the first passenger liner to sail to North America after the war. I joined the long line of people waiting to sign articles for the world cruise and when I arrived at the hatch I announced that I was a chef. I was only twenty at the time, and I suppose I must have looked young and inexperienced. The man at the hatch said 'A wimpy chef,' but he changed his mind when I handed over my credentials. I was offered a choice of jobs and I chose sauce chef, which carried the status of petty officer. When I boarded the great twenty-eight-and-a-half-ton liner and went in search of the two-berth cabin I was entitled to share – the apprentice chefs had to make do with ten-berth accommodation – the sauce chef I was sharing with made the same mistake and told me that 'Apprentices and assistants are down midships.'

My poor mother didn't know anything about this enterprise at all. She thought I'd gone to England for a week's holiday. When I cabled that I was off on a world cruise she went to the police to try to get me back!

The one thing that worried me was that I might get seasick, but thanks be to God that never happened, even in rough seas. And goodness knows the seas were sometimes rough enough. You could be floating along on a sea of glass at one moment, and all of a sudden a storm would erupt. We were in a typhoon for four days at one stage with gales a hundred miles an hour and waves a hundred feet high. Amazing things would happen in a storm at sea – one time

2

a lady was sitting in her bunk having her early morning tea and in the swell a chest of drawers opened, the tray left the top of the bunk and went into the drawer, the drawer closed and not a drop of tea was spilt. And that's true. In the galley we had all sorts of locking devices, also known as Irish guards, to keep the pots on the stoves, and as we moved things around we always had wet tea towels on the surfaces to keep receptacles from sliding.

Another time we had a ship fire that lasted for four days. That was very frightening. The fire was away down in the bowels of the ship where it couldn't be reached. The combustion was caused by two boxes containing Japanese transistors rubbing together.

I got good reports at the end of each voyage and after several cruises I was promoted to assistant chef. I really felt I was getting somewhere now. Some of the men working under me were older than my father. My wildest dreams were realised when I was appointed to the small restaurant on verandah deck overlooking the swimming pool where the elite — lords and ladies, senior army officers and business magnates — dined each night. I catered for about fifty people, and all the meals were individually cooked. I worked there for about ten years, and I suppose it was over this time that I began to think that one day I might set up my own restaurant.

There was a particular captain who befriended me over the years and when he retired he wrote to London suggesting they appoint me executive chef of the whole ship. I was so excited I couldn't sleep until confirmation came from London. Two years later I was appointed to the flagship *Canberra,* where I was responsible for twelve thousand meals and had three hundred people working for me.

I made it my business to get to know the passengers and to make sure they were enjoying their food. Also I always worked in the kitchens alongside my staff. I don't believe in playing the prima donna — I believe a master chef is one who can turn his hand to anything in the kitchen, not just give the orders.

Lord Nuffield, of Morris Minor fame, used to travel religiously with the cricket teams from England to Australia and back again, and he wanted something different for a party he was throwing once. We had already had *foie gras,* cottage loaf filled with fried prawns, smoked salmon stuffed with caviar, and as this was the last party of a six-month voyage he wanted something new and quite different. When the pilot launch brought us out the English newspapers I had the brainwave of serving fish-and-chips in them. His lordship loved the idea. 'The bastards will know they are home,' he chuckled. You should have seen the people in full evening regalia solemnly putting salt and vinegar on their chips!

I used to make it a practice to give cooking demonstrations to the passengers, even before I became executive chef, and I enjoyed it immensely. In fact I have continued to do this all my working life, and I love travelling around the country giving charity demonstrations and meeting and talking to men and women who are interested in good food properly cooked.

It always fascinated the passengers how we could produce the menus we did with fresh produce when we had been at sea for up to two weeks. We had a coldroom for each item of food, even for potatoes, with wooden pallets for air circulation, and my first job every morning was to tour the coldrooms with the storekeeper and butcher, check the thermometers and keep a log book. I take pride in the fact that everything I serve is fresh and I am not a fan of the deep freeze. I once had the ship's surgeon condemn a four-and-a-half-ton consignment of fish because it was freezer burnt. There was a great furore about this because the fishmonger in question had been supplying the company for years and the matter was taken all the way to the chairman.

We used to telex ahead our food orders to all our ports of call and load up when we arrived, but not before I had examined random boxes on the wharf. One lovely morning in Perth I found that the forty tons of cauliflower I had ordered had gone to seed and I told the market gardener that I couldn't cook them. The excited Italian shouted at me that his wife could cook them. Irishmen can wave their arms and shout too and I invited him to take the lot home to her because they weren't coming on my ship. A roar came from above

4

and when we looked up we saw that all unknown to me the passengers were hanging over the rails watching the show.

My first rule of cooking has always been to use perfectly fresh produce. One of my most vivid memories from my days as a trainee at the Gresham is cycling at dawn behind a horse and cart loaded with cabbages on its way to the market. They were stacked in a pyramid which allowed the air to circulate and you can be sure they reached the shops in perfect condition. Supermarket vegetables are often wrapped in plastic wrappings and I would advise against buying them. Food was never meant to be wrapped up like that – it should be allowed to breathe. For best results you should use food in season. Not only is such food more nutritious but it will also taste fresh – a sure sign that food is fresh is that you don't feel bloated after you've eaten it. People often contact me about dinner parties that went wrong and more often than not I find it is not the cooking that is at fault but the produce. Nobody, not even the greatest chef, can produce a good meal if the produce is not in good condition to begin with, the vegetables fresh and the meat properly hung.

Seafaring folk are a breed apart and I certainly enjoyed my years at sea. The company was good to me and gave me opportunities to learn different cuisines by sending me to Tokyo, India, Hong Kong and to the Paris Ritz for a year. In the end, however, I came ashore at home in Ireland and realised my early dream of running my own restaurant though never too far from the sea – first the Mirabeau in Sandycove, County Dublin and now the Waterville Lake Hotel in County Kerry.

People often contact me about their cooking problems and I have enjoyed giving advice on radio, television and in the newspapers, and so at this stage it seems time to put some of my tips and recipes into a book. I find that many people are more daunted by the planning of a meal than by the actual cooking, and that is why this book is arranged in menus rather than in the usual way. Of course you can chop and change these menus to your heart's content, but just remember to plan thoughtfully and to balance your menu carefully – that way you can't go too far wrong.

A NOTE ON QUANTITIES

I'm not a great believer in a lot of fuss about weights and measures. The quantities given in this book will give you an idea of how much of each ingredient you will require, but use your common sense and adjust quantities to suit yourself and your menu. When buying meat calculate in portions – allow about 6–8 oz (about 200g) a head, but remember that when roasting you will lose about a pound of fat to every three pounds of raw meat. By the way, you should not add excess liquid or fat in cooking – food produces its own juice.

I have given metric amounts as well as the more familiar imperial measures. These are only rough equivalents and have been rounded up or down to more convenient amounts and may vary slightly from recipe to recipe. Of course you should stick to one system or the other as amounts are not interchangeable.

A carton of cream in this book means the half-pint (300ml) size, and a small carton is about half that. American readers should note that when we say 'a cup' we are talking about an ordinary teacup and are not using a precise measuring term. Also an American tablespoon is slightly smaller than the Irish one and an American pint contains only 16 fluid ounces, whereas our pint is 20 fluid ounces. The table opposite will help you to work out how much to use, but the differences are not really so great as to throw you out too seriously if you just keep these few facts in mind. Use your judgement.

One other thing – caster sugar is called superfine in America, and when I use 'white sugar' I mean ordinary granulated table sugar.

Irish	American
2 tablespoons	3 tablespoons
2 cups rice*	1½ cups*
1 pint liquid	2½ cups
4 oz butter	½ cup
4 oz flour	1 cup
4 oz sugar	½ cup

*The important thing about rice, regardless of the amount you are cooking, is to get the proportions of rice to water right — use 2 measures of rice to 5 of water, using the same cup or mug to measure both.

BEEF

1 avocado pear
6 prawns
1 tablespoon cream
a little lemon juice
a dash of tabasco
a nip of brandy

Put the prawns in cold water. Bring quickly to the simmer and then chill under a running cold tap before removing shells.

Scoop out the centre of the avocado and blend it with the cream, lemon, tabasco and brandy. Replace the flesh in the avocado shell and serve topped with prawns.

AVOCADO STUFFED WITH PRAWNS

1 fillet of beef (1½ lb; 700g)
8 oz (225g) puff pastry
3 oz (75g) button mushrooms
2 cloves of garlic
a little butter
4 oz (100g) Swiss pâté

10 field mushrooms
1 lb (450g) spinach
a little nutmeg
butter

This is a complicated dish, but such a treat. You have to work to get the combinations right. The beef should be pink and the pastry crispy. It is also expensive, so is best suited to a special occasion.

It is important to seal the beef well with a little oil on a hot pan. Cook it for ten or fifteen minutes so that the blood does not run out of the pastry parcel and spoil the presentation.

Heat the oven to Gas 5 (375°F; 190°C). Toss the sliced button mushrooms in garlic and butter in a pan.

Cream the pâté and smear it over the beef. The pâté gives the beef a wonderful flavour and it won't melt. Then parcel up the beef with the mushrooms in the pastry leaving a little extra room so that the meat won't protrude through the pastry. Pinch it closed along the top and sides in a nice design. Bake until pastry is cooked.

Serve in slices. It is a good idea to clean the knife after each slice so that the effect is not spoilt.

Put a knob of butter on each field mushroom and cook them on a flat tray in a hot oven for just five minutes. For the method of cooking the spinach see page 16.

BEEF WELLINGTON
fillet beef coated in Swiss pâté in a pastry parcel served with field mushrooms and spinach

4 made pancakes (see page 82)
fritter batter
ice cream for two
caster sugar or raspberry jam

Make the pancakes in advance. Put a spoonful of hard ice cream on each cold pancake, folding it over like an envelope. Using a tongs dip the pancake envelope in fritter batter and deep fry in hot oil. Drain on greaseproof paper and serve immediately sprinkled with caster sugar or covered in hot raspberry jam.

FRIED ICE CREAM
ice cream deep fried in pancakes and batter – tastes as amazing as it sounds

Because we are using the best fillet beef in this menu it is rather expensive and so is suitable for that special occasion.

MELON AND PORTWINE

Chill the melons well. Melon tends to pick up flavours and aromas, so wait until the last minute before cutting it and make sure you use a clean knife, not one that has been used for cutting onions or a strongly flavoured vegetable. Cut each melon in half horizontally.

Don't pour in the port before serving. Apart from the fact that everyone does not drink alcohol, portwine stains the fruit which does not look well, so serve it on the side.

This could equally well be served as a dessert.

2 honeydew melons
1 glass portwine

BEEF STROGONOFF
served on a bed of turmeric-flavoured rice

Cut the beef into thin strips and chop the onion and garlic finely. Sauté the garlic and onion for two to four minutes on a very hot pan with the butter, add the mushrooms without their stalks. Dust the beef in flour and paprika and sauté off until brown. Pour in the white wine and at the last moment add the sour cream.

Serve on a bed of turmeric-flavoured rice, sprinkle with chopped parsley. . . and there you have it. To make turmeric rice simply add the turmeric to the rice when cooking.

2 lb (900g) fillet beef
1 onion
1 clove of garlic
2–3 oz (50–75g) mushrooms
a little flour
4 tablespoons butter
1 cup white wine
1 cup sour cream (see page 98)
1 tablespoon paprika
parsley to garnish

2 cups rice
½ teaspoon turmeric

CROQUE MONSIEUR
a cheese and ham savoury

This could be served as a starter, but we don't want to kill the flavour of the beef with a heavy appetiser. It would also make a nice supper dish.

Butter the bread on each side and toast it. Trim off all the crusts and make sandwiches with the toast, the Gruyère and the ham and deep fry in hot fat. The cheese will melt and seal the sandwiches. Sprinkle with paprika.

8 slices buttered white bread
4 slices Gruyère cheese
4 slices cooked ham
a little paprika

STEAK AND KIDNEY PIE

¼ lb (100g) kidneys
¾ lb (350g) stewing beef
1 cup of brown stock or water
4 onions
a little butter
a little flour
mixed herbs
parsley
1 egg
8 oz (225g) pastry*

Simple and straightforward. My only rule for this dish is that the two meats should be cooked separately.

Quarter the kidneys after you've blanched them (see note on kidneys page 84) and sauté them with the finely chopped onion.

Cut the beef into small cubes and sauté with plenty of onions in another pan with the parsley and mixed herbs. Add a knob of butter and dust the mixture with flour. Moisten with the stock or water.

Turn the steak and kidney into a pie dish and cover with puff pastry.

Brush with beaten egg and bake until brown at gas mark 5 (375°F; 190°C).

A variation on this is steak, kidney and mushroom pie. Simply add sautéed sliced mushrooms to the dish before you cover with pastry.

SPICED APPLE CRUMBLE

4 apples
1 tablespoon water
a little sugar
2 oz (50g) butter or marg
4 oz (100g) flour
½ teaspoon mixed spice

The apple crumble should be put into the oven half an hour before you serve the steak and kidney pie.

Core, peel and chop the apples into quite small pieces, and three-quarters fill a buttered dish. Add a tablespoon of water.

Make the crumble by mixing the butter with the flour and spices.

Strew this over the apples and bake until brown.

*Potato can be used instead of pastry

BRAISED STEAK AND ONIONS
served with mashed potatoes

This is what I call soulfood. It is a family dish, easy to prepare and cook. Rump steak is best. Ask the butcher to cut it up into pieces about three inches by four. You could braise the whole piece but it's better to cut the steaks, as they are easier to handle. Cut the onions in half rings rather than whole. They don't look as well but they are easier to manage when eating.

Season the steak pieces.

Use a hot pan or skillet on top of the stove and seal the steak in it with a little oil. Then put the meat in a casserole. Make a brown sauce with the residue of the pan. First pour off any excess fat and then make the sauce. Add a knob of butter and finely chopped onion and garlic to the residue and sauté. Dust with flour to make a roux and break down the consistency with the stock. Pour the sauce over the sealed steak making sure you have plenty. It shouldn't be too thick because it will thicken as it reduces.

To prevent the casserole from going dry place it in a pan of hot water. Leave it to bake for two hours or until tender in a slow oven.

Next sauté the onions cut in half rings and serve with the braised steak. Boil the potatoes and mash them with a little hot milk; serve on the side.

1½ lb (700g) rump steak
4 oz (100g) butter
2 cloves of garlic
½ onion
a little flour
seasoning
beef stock

4 onions
8 medium potatoes

APPLES AND CHEESE

You would not want a filling dessert after this, so round off with crunchy apples and a piece of cheese.

This is a robust Sunday lunch. The salad and the apple pie can be prepared in advance, and the main course won't tax the brain too much and leaves plenty of time for reading the Sunday papers.

MENU FOR 4

FRESH SALAD

small head of lettuce, chicory or Chinese leaves
4 tomatoes
a sprig of fennel
lemon juice or oil and vinegar dressing

This can be eaten as a refreshing starter, or you can serve it on the side if you like.

Shred the leaves with your hands, not a knife, crisp in icy water, shake well and refrigerate for fifteen minutes in a sealed plastic bag.

Chop the tomatoes into segments and cut the fennel finely. Serve with lemon juice or an oil and vinegar dressing.

PRIME ROAST BEEF
with horseradish sauce, served with red cabbage and roast potatoes

8 oz (225g) of prime beef per adult portion

1 head red cabbage
½ cup water
½ cup malt vinegar
1 large cooking apple

shop horseradish sauce
1 tablespoon cream
parsley
8–9 potatoes

Roast the beef in a preheated medium oven, allowing twenty minutes to the pound and twenty minutes over.

Shred the cabbage. Spread it out on the kitchen table, season well and leave it for half an hour. Put it in an ovenproof dish with the water and the vinegar and the apple cut up into pieces. Cover with greaseproof paper and cook in the oven (medium) for fifteen minutes.

Fresh horseradish is difficult to get, but you can use the shop sauce. Strain the radish out of the bought sauce, taking all the bitterness out of it, and then simply fold the pieces in fresh cream and sprinkle with parsley.

'Roast' potatoes are best parboiled in their jackets, peeled and browned on a hot pan rather than cooked in the oven. This way they are not hard on the outside and hollow in the middle.

APPLE PIE À LA MODE

apple pie
ice cream
raspberry jam (optional)

This is just apple pie and ice cream, a simple dessert which pleases most palates and so is a 'safe' choice. Use fresh cooking apples in the pie. For variation serve hot jam sauce on the side. This is simply heated raspberry jam.

Quite a straightforward menu. The starter can be prepared and served in a matter of minutes and the dessert can be prepared in advance.

GARLIC MUSHROOMS

Trim the mushrooms and wipe with a dry cloth. Leave them whole. Sauté the onion and garlic (very finely chopped) on a hot pan with the oil and butter. Stir in the mushrooms. Season with freshly ground black pepper and serve with toast and garnished with parsley and if liked a little parmesan.

1 lb (450g) button mushrooms
3 cloves of garlic
1 large onion
4 oz (100g) butter
1 tablespoon oil
black pepper
parsley and a little parmesan cheese for garnishing
some triangles of toast

POTROAST
with vegetables and boiled potatoes

Seal the rump of beef well on the top of the stove in a hot pan with a little oil.

Take the meat out and put it in a casserole. Then make a roux with the butter and flour and break down the consistency with the stock and/or red wine. Make plenty because the cooking process is long. Pour the sauce over the meat and bake it in the oven for three to four hours at gas mark 3 (325°F; 170°C) with the lid on.

For best results place the casserole in a bain marie: put enough boiling water in a tray to cover the sides of the casserole. Don't forget to replenish the water as it evaporates.

Ten minutes before serving sauté your vegetables, finely chopped, on the pan and add to the casserole.

Boil the potatoes in their jackets. Drain when cooked and for a lovely fluffy potato place a dry clean teatowel on top of them for a few minutes before serving.

1½ lb (700g) rump of beef
2 pints (1 litre) brown stock
¼ pint (150 ml) red wine (optional)
a little flour
some butter or margarine
1 onion
1 stick of celery
½ red pepper
½ green pepper
2 carrots

9 potatoes

PEARS HILARY

Poach the pears whole in a little water and sugar. Peel carefully, leaving the stem intact. Serve in individual dishes covered with fresh cream and grated chocolate with little macaroons on the side.

4 pears
a little sugar
a small carton of cream
2 oz (50g) grated chocolate
8–12 macaroons

MENU FOR 1

6–12 snails
2–3 cloves of garlic
a little butter

Snails, which you buy at a delicatessan, are no trouble to cook. All you have to do is put the snails and their shells into the oven with some crushed garlic, hard knobs of butter and bake together until the butter is a lovely nutty colour.

When ready to serve garnish with chopped parsley.

ESCARGOTS NATURE
snails baked in the oven with garlic butter

4–6 oz (100–175g) fillet beef
pepper and salt
1 egg yolk
½ onion
anchovies, capers, gherkins

An acquired taste, this is, however, a delicious and interesting dish. Try it some time when you are on your own.

The beef should be cut up very finely, not minced, and seasoned as desired.

Presentation is very important in this classical dish. Place the egg yolk in a hollow in the centre of the portion of meat and criss-cross with anchovies. Serve the capers, chopped gherkins and finely chopped onion on the side.

The dish is eaten by binding the ingredients to suit your palate with the egg yolk.

STEAK TARTARE
lean beef eaten raw

lettuce
oil and vinegar dressing

You can have the salad on the side, or in true French fashion as another course. See page 13 for tips on salad making.

GREEN SALAD

On its own the ox tongue and spinach would do as a brunch or light lunch, or it can be fortified with potatoes and a dessert.

MENU FOR 4

OX TONGUE AND FRESH SPINACH
with baked potatoes and chopped chives

You will probably need two tongues for four people. It is not normal to eat the neck part.

This dish is cooked in the same way as corned beef. Put a little Colman's mustard in the cooking water to give it a sweet-and-sour flavour and boil the tongue for twenty minutes to the pound and twenty minutes over. When the little bubbles appear on the skin – the tongue actually appears through a little hole – it is cooked.

Serve cut into fairly thick slices. If the slices are too thin tongue is inclined to dry up in a matter of minutes.

Shred the spinach, removing any tough leaves or stems. Wash well and shake. Cook in a pot for a few minutes with a knob of butter – no need to add water. Sprinkle with a little nutmeg and serve.

Bake the potatoes on a bed of salt for extra flavour and serve with chopped chives.

1–2 ox tongues
Colman's mustard

1–2 lbs (450–900g) fresh spinach
a little butter
grated nutmeg

8 potatoes
chopped chives

FRESH FRUIT SALAD

Make the salad by chopping fresh fruit as available. Apples and oranges are quite acceptable and preferable to tinned fruits. If you are using apples or bananas sprinkle a little lemon juice on them to keep them from discolouring. This looks well served in the shell of half a grapefruit – you can add the segments to the other fruits.

fresh fruit as available
lemon juice
2 grapefruit (optional)

An old favourite, cottage pie is a meal in itself really, but you could serve it with peas or cabbage or even both if you like. It's ideal for lunch or supper, with or without a pudding.

COTTAGE PIE

MENU FOR 4

1 clove of garlic
1 large onion
a little butter or oil
1½ lb (700g) minced round steak
2 dessertspoons tomato ketchup
8 potatoes
egg to glaze

You can omit the onions if you're cooking this for finicky children, or you could chop the onions very finely so they can't be picked out by tiny fingers and placed on the side of the plate with disdain. I prefer to use fresh mince rather than leftovers.

Sauté the garlic and onion first in butter or oil and then brown the meat gently on the same pan. Put into a hot oven for ten to fifteen minutes. Then add the tomato ketchup.

Mash the potatoes until fluffy and cover the meat with the mash. Smooth with a fork, glaze with beaten egg and bake at gas mark 5 (375°F; 190°C) until golden brown – about twenty minutes.

BAKED APPLE MERINGUE PIE

4 big cooking apples and sugar to taste
2 egg whites
4 oz (100g) sugar

It is very satisfying to use the oven to its full capacity, so baked apple meringue pie makes an ideal pudding to go with cottage pie.

Peel, core and quarter the apples. Blanch for a few minutes with sugar to taste until soft but not mushy and put in an ovenproof dish.

Make the meringue by whisking the egg whites until stiff. Then whisk in half of the sugar, whisk again and finally whisk in the rest of the sugar. Cover the apple with the meringue mixture and return to the oven to bake until crisp and golden brown – about ten to fifteen minutes.

BEEF GOULASH
with rice or baked
potatoes

A fortifying stew which benefits from long slow cooking. This method is used for all kinds of stew.

Cut the rump steak into small square pieces, removing all fat.

Heat enough oil to cover the bottom of the pan and sauté the onion, finely cut celery, carrot and garlic and brown the meat with them on the hot pan. Then put the contents of the pan into a casserole.

Now make a sauce from the residue of the pan by adding a knob of butter to it, dusting with flour and breaking down the consistency with beef stock. Pour this over the casserole, place the casserole in a bain marie (tray of hot water) and cook in a slow oven for three to four hours until the meat is tender. Don't forget to replenish the water in the bain marie or it will dry out.

Before serving, sauté the extra vegetables on the pan for a few minutes, fold through the goulash and cook for a further ten minutes.

For extra colour add peas or French beans.

Serve with plain boiled rice (see page 72) or baked potatoes.

1½–2 lb (700–900g) rump beef
for sauce
1 onion
1 stick of celery
1 carrot
1 clove of garlic
½ pint (300ml) beef stock
a little flour
a little butter
extra vegetables
2 sticks of celery
1 onion
2 carrots
peas or French beans (optional)

2 cups of long-grain rice
or
9 potatoes

BANANA FRITTERS

These are cooked in the same way as apple fritters (see page 21) using whole bananas.

4–8 bananas
fritter batter (see page 82)

An economical menu which uses inexpensive ingredients and makes good use of the oven.

OXTAIL
with mashed potatoes

MENU FOR 4

2–3 oxtails
1 clove of garlic
½ onion
a little flour
a drop of red wine (optional)
4 carrots
1 small turnip
12 button onions

7–9 potatoes mashed

This dish benefits greatly from long slow cooking.

The butcher will cut the oxtails into knuckles for you. Put them in a dish and bake in a slow oven for several hours – some people leave them overnight – to remove all the fat. The fat will rise to the top and you can spoon it off. You will find that the oxtails will shrink considerably.

When ready take the meat from the dish and take the meat off the bones. Now make a brown beef stock out of the bones. Use the residue to make a sauce – add a knob of butter and as it bubbles up sauté some finely chopped garlic and onion in it, dust with flour and break down the consistency with the brown stock. A drop of red wine enhances the flavour of oxtail. Season to taste.

Put the oxtails back in the casserole covered with the sauce and return to the oven for another two or three hours. A good tip is to put a little flour-and-water paste in the hole in the lid of your casserole to prevent steam escaping and the meat from drying out.

Cut the vegetables into thin two-inch strips – but leave the onions whole – sauté them and add to the casserole ten minutes before serving. (This is known as jardinière vegetables, by the way.)

Serve with mashed potatoes (see page 12) on the side.

BAKED APPLES
with custard or jubilee sauce

4 big cooking apples
1 oz (25g) butter
1 tablespoon honey
a handful of raisins or a few cloves
1 pint custard
or jubilee sauce (see page 98)

Baked apples go well with oxtail because the apples can cook in the oven at the same time as the meat. Choose large apples. Wash and core them and in the hole in the centre put a knob of butter, a spoon of honey and a few raisins or cloves. Bake in the slow oven for three-quarters of an hour.

Make up the custard and pour over the baked apples. Jubilee sauce would go well instead of custard for a nice toffee-apple effect.

An expensive menu, definitely for a special occasion. The lobster bisque is a little complicated, but the steak dish is relatively straight-forward and the apple fritters can be prepared in advance, so all you have to do is dip the prepared fruit in the batter and cook.

MENU FOR 2

LOBSTER BISQUE

Put the lobster into cold water alive and put a heavy weight on the pot. The lobster must be alive – a dead lobster is poisonous – and if you put it into boiling water the flesh will be tough. By the time the cold water comes to the boil the lobster has gone to sleep and feels no pain.

Remove the lobster when the shell has turned bright red and keep the stock. Don't boil it as fish stock becomes bitter if over-boiled.

Sauté the chopped garlic, fennel, peppers, celery and onion on a very hot pan until brown with a little butter, margarine or oil.

Add a little flour very gently, to bind the vegetables together and make a roux, stirring all the time in a figure-of-eight. When the vegetables congregate in the centre of the saucepan you have the right consistency. Add the concassed (i.e. blanched, skinned and chopped) tomatoes. They add colour and act as a thickener. Add the lobster stock gradually, breaking down the consistency. The soup is right when it masks the back of the ladle. Now let it simmer for five minutes. Finally add a few little pieces of butter to stop a skin forming.

Now remove the lobster meat from the shell, sauté it lightly in a little butter on a hot pan to bring out the flavour and add to the soup. Keep the remainder of the stock in case the bisque thickens too much. Serve with a nip of brandy and cream.

1 small live lobster
½ red pepper
½ green pepper
1 clove of garlic
½ onion
1 stick of celery
a sprig of fennel
2 tomatoes
a little flour
butter
a nip of brandy
a little cream

STEAK DIANE
served with cauliflower
and sautéed potatoes

The steaks should be very thin, so beat them gently if they are too thick. Dust lightly with mustard and seal on a hot pan with a little oil.

Add the finely chopped onion and garlic to the pan with a knob of butter and sauté. Add the sliced mushrooms, a dash of Worcester sauce, a nip of brandy and a tablespoonful of cream and serve immediately.

2 sirloin steaks
Colman's mustard
4 mushrooms
½ onion
clove of garlic
a little red wine
1 tablespoon cream
butter
dash of Worcester sauce

CAULIFLOWER MORNAY

1 small cauliflower
½ lemon
a little flour
a little butter
½ cup grated cheddar cheese

4–5 cooked potatoes

To make the cauliflower mornay make a funnel in the stalk of the cauliflower. This way you can cook it whole and break it into pieces later. Cook in boiling water with a half a lemon in the pot to keep the cauliflower white. You'll know it's cooked when the stalks become bright green.

Make the mornay sauce with the cauliflower stock rather than with milk, as the stock contains lots of nutrition. Make a roux in the normal way and add the stock. Don't allow the stock to boil, as it smells strongly. As soon as the sauce is made add the grated cheese.

For the sautéed potatoes use cold potatoes that have been boiled in their jackets. Peel them and slice them neatly and cook on a hot pan with a little fat until golden brown.

APPLE FRITTERS

1 large cooking apple
fritter batter
a little lemon juice
a pinch of salt
a little flour
caster sugar

Make fritter batter as described on page 82. Make the batter well in advance to give it a chance to ferment.

Peel the apples, core them and cut into thick slices. Put them in cold water with a pinch of salt and a little lemon juice to prevent browning.

When you come to cook the fritters, pat the apple slices dry, dip in flour and then in batter, making sure to let the excess batter run off the fruit so you don't end up with a thick ball of batter to munch through. Deep fry one or two at a time in hot oil, toss on greaseproof paper, sprinkle with caster sugar and serve immediately.

POULTRY

4 eggs
1 spring onion (scallion)
2 tomatoes
a little pepper
homemade mayonnaise
a lettuce heart

Boil, shell and halve the eggs. Scoop out the yolk and blend with the finely chopped spring onion and tomato concasse – tomatoes blanched, skinned and roughly chopped. Season with pepper and add a little homemade mayonnaise (see page 96). Replace the mixture in the egg whites and serve on heart of lettuce leaves.

STUFFED EGGS
served on heart of lettuce leaves

1 x 3 lb (1.5kg) chicken
bouquet garni
6 sticks of celery
2 onions
4 carrots
1 clove of garlic
a knob of butter
a little flour
1 glass red wine
extra vegetables
3 sticks of celery
1 onion
2 carrots
12 mushrooms
1 clove of garlic
2 rashers
a little butter or marg
8–9 potatoes

The secret of a good casserole is to cook some of the vegetables separately and add them to the dish just before serving so they are nice and crunchy.

Roast the chicken in the normal way, leaving a trace of moisture in it. Remove from the oven and allow to cool before removing the meat from the bone.

To make your stock put the carcase of the chicken in a pot of cold water with bouquet garni and half the vegetables and bring to the boil.

Heat up the residue in the roasting dish and as it bubbles up add a knob of butter. Sauté the garlic and the remaining vegetables for three to four minutes in this and then dust with flour to make a roux. Gradually add the heated red wine and stir to a creamy consistency. Add the stock slowly, leave to simmer for five to ten minutes and then cool, adding a little butter to keep a skin from forming. Cook the extra vegetables in a little water with a nut of butter to give them a nice glaze.

Now put the chicken in the casserole dish and strain the sauce over it. Then place the casserole in a deepish tray of hot water. Leave to heat gently in a medium oven for about ten minutes, by which time your extra vegetables should be cooked. Strain these, sauté the strips of bacon and add the lot to the casserole.

Serve with potatoes baked on a tray of salt.

CHICKEN CASSEROLE
with a baked potato to mop up the sauce

4 oranges
a nip of Grand Marnier
cream

Simply peel the oranges, slice in circles and soak in the liqueur. Serve with whipped cream on the side.

ORANGES IN GRAND MARNIER

Here's a quick summer's menu.

PRAWN COCKTAIL

The secret of prawn cocktail is the sauce. Make this by whipping the cream until stiff and adding a nip of brandy and enough tomato ketchup to colour.

Prawn cocktail is usually spoiled by bales of grass in the bottom of the glass. Simply lay the prawns on lettuce heart leaves and serve the sauce on the side with wedges of lemon and brown bread and butter.

8 oz (225g) cooked and peeled prawns
lettuce heart
a small carton of cream
a nip of brandy
a little tomato ketchup
lemon to garnish
brown bread and butter

CHICKEN BREASTS TURMERIC
served on a bed of fluffy rice

Chicken breasts with a delicate sauce made from the chicken stock and coloured with turmeric.

Put the chicken breasts in cold water with the bouquet of vegetables. Bring the water to a simmer. When cooked — about fifteen minutes — remove the chicken breasts and put to one side, covering with wet greaseproof paper to keep the moisture in. Keep the stock on the heat.

To make the sauce put a knob of butter into a saucepan and heat. Do not allow it to clarify. Then add a little flour, exactly as you do when making a roux. Stir in a figure-of-eight and gradually add the strained, boiling stock until you have the right consistency. The stock must be boiling, otherwise the sauce will be lumpy. Colour it with the turmeric, which gives it a lovely piquancy. Keep back a little stock to heat up the chicken and then mask the breasts with the sauce and serve on a bed of fluffy rice (see page 72). Garnish with parsley.

4 chicken breasts
bouquet of vegetables (celery, carrots, onion etc)
a knob of butter
flour
½ teaspoon turmeric
parsley to garnish

2 cups long-grain rice

RASPBERRY FOOL

This is an old favourite and it makes a small amount of fruit go a long way.

Keep a few berries for decoration, sugar the rest to taste and mix with most of the cream whipped. You can purée the fruit with the cream, but I prefer it with a bite in it so I leave the fruit whole. Chill. Make up the custard quite thickly and allow to go cold.

When ready to serve, fold the lot together and decorate with the remaining whipped cream and whole raspberries.

¾ lb (350g) fresh raspberries
a small carton of cream
about 2 oz (50g) sugar
1 pint (600ml) custard

SEAFOOD PLATE
with rosemary sauce

enough of the following
seafoods to allow everyone a
little of each: smoked
salmon, cooked lobster, crab
and shrimp pieces
lettuce heart
lemon to garnish
1 cup whipped cream
a dash of tabasco
a nip of brandy
a pinch of rosemary

The seafood plate consists of the listed seafoods or as many of them as you like served on heart of lettuce leaves garnished with lemon and with rosemary sauce on the side. To make the sauce simply add the tabasco and brandy to the whipped cream with a pinch of rosemary. Do not prepare the seafood too far in advance and do not refrigerate it.

CHICKEN MARYLAND
served with fruit and corn fritters

4 boneless chicken portions
homemade breadcrumbs
egg wash (beaten egg mixed
a little milk)
to garnish
apple fritters
banana fritters
pineapple fritters
corn fritters
4 rashers of bacon
4 tomatoes

This dish takes a bit of preparing, but the actual cooking won't take more than fifteen minutes.

Dust the chicken portions in flour, dip in the eggwash and coat with breadcrumbs. Then deep fry in hot fat.

After removing from the pan put in a medium oven for a few minutes to ensure it's cooked right through.

Bake the tomatoes whole, wrapped in the rashers. Make your various fruit fritters (as for apple fritters on page 21) and your corn fritters (see below) and garnish the chicken with these and the tomatoes wrapped in bacon.

CORN FRITTERS

2 oz (50g) flour
a pinch of pepper
1 egg
1/8 pint (3 fl. oz; 75ml) milk
a small can of corn

To make the batter sift the flour and pepper into a bowl, drop the egg into a well in the centre and add the milk slowly, mixing all the time, until you have a smooth consistency.

Strain the corn and add to the batter mixture.

Spoon the mixture onto a hot pan with a little oil (throw off any excess) and cook until golden brown on both sides.

FRESH PEARS IN PORTWINE

4 pears
1 cup of portwine

Blanch the pears for ten to fifteen minutes in boiling water. Then peel carefully leaving the stem on and marinate in portwine. Half an hour will do.

Serve whole and baste with the marinade.

SMOKED SALMON
with melon

For each serving use a wedge of melon with a thin slice of smoked salmon over it. Garnish with lemon.

smoked salmon
melon
sugar
lemon

ROAST DUCKLING
with sweet and sour sauce served with roast potatoes and crispy cabbage

Duckling needs a lot of care, otherwise it is fatty and difficult to digest. This very old recipe never fails.

First roast the duck in a medium oven, gas mark 4 (350°F; 180°C) for approximately twenty to the pound. You can tell a duck is cooked when the 'parson's nose' becomes pointy.

When cooked remove it from the dish, allow to cool and take it off the bone. Put your fingers inside the neck cavity of the duck and pull out the V-shaped wishbone. Using the fingers, pull off first one leg and then the other. Using the fingers, pull the bone from the centre of the thigh. Put the thigh meat on a platter skin side up. Pull the leg meat from the bone. Put this skin side up on the platter. Grab the upper end of the side of the breast and pull down. The duck breast half – both meat and skin – should come off in one piece. Pull off the opposite piece of breast meat. The duck skin may be dotted with butter and the pieces put in a very low oven to keep warm.

Then, to get rid of the excess fat, place the meat in another dish and put in a very hot oven gas mark 7 (425°F; 220°C) for another ten minutes.

Serve with a clear sweet and sour sauce made by mixing the sauce ingredients together and heating through. That's it. No thickening is necessary.

Serve with roast potatoes (see page 13) and crispy cabbage.

1 large duckling
sauce
1 eggcup orange juice
1 eggcup Worcester sauce
1 cup red wine
a nip of brandy
8–9 potatoes

CRISPY CABBAGE

Crispy cabbage just takes minutes. Cook the tender heart leaves only in a little boiling water with a knob butter for about three minutes. Strain and serve.

cabbage hearts
knob of butter

1 x 8 inch half plain sponge cake
fruit juice to moisten
fresh fruit salad to taste
1 block of ice cream (1 pint; 600ml)
6 egg whites
a little sugar
a nip of brandy

BAKED ALASKA

Pre-heat the oven first to gas mark 7 (425°F, 220°C). Soak the sponge in fruit juice, just enough to moisten it rather than make it flabby. Next add a bed of fresh fruit salad. Top that with ice cream.

Beat the egg whites to a stiff meringue and carefully cover the entire cake base and ice cream.

Put half an eggshell on top of the alaska, open side up, camouflaging it with the meringue. It will come out of the oven piping hot and make it easy to flame the brandy. Put the alaska in the oven to brown (about five minutes). In the meantime heat the brandy, but do not boil or it will evaporate.

When the meringue is ready pour the brandy into the shell and light it. Tilt it left and right as you go to the table and it will flame magnificently.

One last tip – have a jug of hot water beside you when you are serving the alaska to dip the serving spoon in between servings. This prevents it getting sticky.

HORS D'OEUVRE

Presentation is very important. Serve a little of whatever you fancy — tuna, stuffed egg, coleslaw and stuffed tomato, for instance. You can serve just one of these, or a selection. Other suitable starters would be sardines on toast, egg mayonnaise or pâté on toast.

ROAST PARTRIDGE
with breadcrumbs, bread sauce and game chips

This is exotic but really quite straightforward. Of course it tastes twice as nice if you've shot it yourself. Make sure the game is hung by the legs.

The main problem people tell me they have with game is that it tends to go dry in the cooking, so when cooking your partridge I suggest you put a few cloves of garlic in the centre and cover the bird with streaky rashers to protect it from the heat of the oven. Preheat the oven to gas mark 7 (425°F; 220°C).

Put the bird on a layer of vegetables — carrots, onion, celery, roughly chopped — in a baking tray and roast. Depending on size it should cook in twenty to thirty mintues in a hot oven. It should be medium cooked, not rare. Lower the heat of the oven for the last ten minutes and five minutes before the bird is cooked remove the bacon to crisp the skin.

Make a sauce with the residue of the dish by adding a drop of Madeira and a little cream. Strain. No flour is added, so this has a lovely delicate taste.

1 or 2 partridges
2–3 cloves of garlic
a few streaky rashers of bacon
a bouquet of vegetables — celery, onion, carrots
a drop of Madeira
a little cream

BREAD SAUCE

For the bread sauce stick three or four cloves into a small onion and simmer it in the milk. Meanwhile soak bread without crusts in milk to make a gruel. Strain off the excess milk. Add this gruel to the hot milk — remove the onion of course first — with a little salt, pepper and nutmeg.

As well as bread sauce partridge is always served with breadcrumbs and game chips. Put fresh breadcrumbs in the oven with little knobs of butter and bake until crisp.

3 slices of white bread
1 cup of milk and a little extra
1 onion
3–4 cloves of garlic
a little nutmeg

1 cup breadcrumbs
a little butter

GAME CHIPS

Game chips should be cut thinly. Blanch them in medium hot fat and remove. Reheat the fat until it is very hot, toss in the chips again to crisp them up. Drain on greaseproof paper and sprinkle with salt.

4 potatoes

2 celery hearts 2 streaky rashers a little butter a drop of Madeira	Cut the sticks in four. Cook in the oven with the streaky rashers, a little water, a knob of butter and a drop of Madeira for half an hour. Remove the rashers before serving.	**BRAISED CELERY**
2 pears ice cream for two 3 oz (75g) cooking chocolate	Place the ice cream in individual glasses. Fresh peeled pears are placed on top and hot melted chocolate poured over them just before serving.	**PEARS HÉLÈNE**

Not as expensive as it sounds. Turkey is one of the cheapest meats around with little waste, and the bones make great soup afterwards.

MENU FOR 6

STUFFED CORNETS OF SMOKED SALMON
with prawns and Blarney sauce

I've adapted this recipe from the exotic cornucopia where caviar is used for stuffing. It is quite delicious, but with the price of caviar, I think we'll stick to our own Blarney. Roll the salmon into cones and fill with the prawns. To make the sauce whip unsweetened cream with enough tabasco to taste and a nip of brandy. Colour with tomato ketchup and serve on the side.

6 slices smoked salmon
8 oz (225g) prawns cooked and peeled
a small carton of cream
a dash of tabasco
a nip of brandy
a little tomato ketchup

ROAST TURKEY
with cranberry sauce and stuffing

Preheat the oven for fifteen minutes to gas mark 5 (375°F; 190°C). Cover the roasting pan with a thin film of oil and sit the turkey in it on a light bed of celery, onion etc. Sprinkle with salt. Do not tie the legs together as this prevents the natural juices from being absorbed and you end up with that portion of the bird uncooked.

Baste every twenty minutes or so for a lovely crispy effect. Allow twenty minutes to the pound when cooking. The best way to judge if the bird is done is by checking its progress. If the wings are crispy, the 'parson's nose' is pointy and the legs protrude through the skin, its ready for eating.

Serve with stuffing, cranberry sauce, brussel sprouts and roast potatoes (see page 13).

Make an X-incision at the stalk end of each sprout. Pop them into boiling water with a knob of butter which gives a nice sheen. Don't overcook – they are best with a little 'bone' in them.

1 x 10 lb (4–5k) turkey
bouquet of vegetables –
celery, carrots, onions
salt

2 lb (1 kg) brussel sprouts
a little butter
9 potatoes

CRANBERRY SAUCE

Dissolve the sugar in the boiling water, add the cranberries and simmer. Serve hot or cold.

4 oz (100g) sugar
4 oz (100g) cranberries
¼ pint (100ml) water

STUFFING

This can be eaten hot or cold or even served on toast. It tastes like pâté. I never put the stuffing inside the bird. I feel it is unhygienic – any blood which has remained could become embedded in it.

Mix the potatoes with the sausage meat. Sauté the finely chopped onion and sage or thyme on a hot pan with a knob of butter for a few minutes. Then add it to the potatoes and sausage meat. Mix well until you have a creamy consistency. Pour some beautiful fat from

12 oz (300g) sausage meat
4 oz (100g) dry mashed potato
a pinch of sage or thyme
a little butter

the turkey to moisten a dish and turn in the stuffing. Cover with a sheet of greaseproof paper.

Bake in a hot oven for twenty minutes.

6 made pancakes
ice cream
Cointreau
6 oz (150g) cooking chocolate

PANCAKES
with ice cream and chocolate sauce

Another variation of the adaptable pancake. Make thin pancakes in advance. Add a dash of Cointreau to each scoop of ice cream. Place in the centre of the pancake and fold. Cover with hot chocolate sauce – simply melted cooking chocolate.

The chicken dish is unusual and, when avocados are in season, economical. It could also be served on its own for lunch or supper. **MENU FOR 4**

SEAFOOD PANCAKES

Seafood pancakes sound expensive and indeed they can be adapted to serve as a main course. Here we are simply using them as an appetiser and so we use smaller quantities.

Make four thin pancakes (see page 82).

Poach the scallops and the prawns separately. Throw out the scallop stock, as it is bitter, but keep the prawn stock. Then slice the scallops and mix with the sieved boiled egg and prawns.

Sauté the finely chopped onion and the mushrooms in butter and blend in flour to make a roux.

Add the prawn stock to break down the consistency, thinning with cream if necessary.

Season and add the scallops, eggs and prawns.

Cook for five minutes stirring all the time and then place a spoonful of the mixture on each pancake and fold envelope-style.

Save a little of the sauce to spoon over the pancakes. Sprinkle with a little parmesan on top and grill until brown.

4 made pancakes
2 scallops
1 cup of prawns, trimmed and peeled
1 boiled egg
½ onion
6 mushrooms
1 oz (25g) flour
2 oz (50g) butter
¼ pint (150 ml) cream
a little parmesan

CHICKEN AND AVOCADO IN CREAM
served with fluffy rice

Cut the chicken into strips – you should get about seven from each chicken breast. Have the pan very hot. Add the butter, shallots, mushrooms and then your chicken pieces. Stir gently with a wooden spoon until the chicken is cooked – about five minutes.

Add the brandy and cream and sprinkle the peeled avocado cut into strips over the chicken before serving.

Serve rice on the side (see page 72).

1½ lb (700g) boneless breast of chicken
2 tablespoons butter or margarine
1 tablespoon freshly chopped shallots
¼ lb (100g) sliced mushrooms
2 tablespoons cognac
1½ cups double cream
1 avocado

2 cups long-grain rice

BLACK GRAPES AND MELON BALLS

Remove stones from grapes and scoop the melon flesh into balls. Marinate the fruit in orange juice and Grand Marnier. Chill. Serve in individual glasses with the marinade poured over them.

melon
4 oz (100g) black grapes
juice of 1–2 oranges
a nip of Grand Marnier

MUSHROOM SOUP

6 oz (175g) mushrooms
a little butter
a little flour
½ onion
2 sticks of celery
1 clove of garlic
1 pint (570ml) chicken stock
a little cream

Sauté the sliced mushrooms separately and remove them from the pan. Now make the roux by sautéing the garlic, onion and celery, finely chopped, in butter. Bind with flour and break down the consistency with the heated chicken stock.

Heat the mushrooms in cream and spoon some into each bowl. Pour the strained stock over them.

CHICKEN BREASTS AND FRIED RICE

2 cups rice
4 chicken breasts
bouquet of vegetables
(celery, carrot, onion etc)
a little butter or oil
1 clove of garlic
½ green pepper
½ red pepper
a handful of mushrooms
2 egg yolks
parsley to garnish

First cook the rice in the usual way (page 72).

Put the chicken breasts into cold water with a little bouquet of vegetables – carrots, celery, onion, whatever you happen to have – to make a stock. When the water begins to simmer remove from the heat and save the stock for another time.

Now cut up the pepper and mushrooms and sauté in a little oil or butter along with the chopped garlic.

Slice the chicken breasts into scallop shapes and add to the vegetable pan with the cooked rice. Fold all the ingredients together with the unbeaten egg yolks.

Sprinkle with parsley to serve.

LAYERED RHUBARB CRUMBLE

1–2 lb (500–900g) rhubarb
4 oz (100g) homemade
breadcrumbs
3 oz (75g) shredded suet
3 oz (75g) brown sugar
1 teaspoon cinnamon
a little butter

Layer half the rhubarb, trimmed and cut into two-inch pieces, on a greased ovenproof dish. Mix all the other ingredients except the butter together to make the crumble and sprinkle half of it over the fruit. Now layer the rest of the fruit on top and finally sprinkle the remaining crumble on top of that again. Dot with butter and bake in a moderate oven until the fruit is soft and the topping golden.

33

PORK

This is a very easy menu. The soup has to be prepared in advance, but the main course cooks very quickly and the dessert is simplicity itself.

MENU FOR 4

2 cups split peas
1 ham bone
1¾ pints (1 litre) chicken stock
fried bread

Soak the split peas overnight. Then place in a medium oven submerged in water with the ham bone in the centre to cook for a few hours.

When the peas are cooked make a soup using chicken stock to break down the thick pea purée.

Strip the ham bone and put the chopped meat back into the soup. Serve with croutons made from fried diced bread sprinkled on top.

PEA SOUP
with croutons

2 pork steaks
8 mushrooms
1 onion
1 clove of garlic
a little cream
paprika

2 cups rice
a red cabbage
a little malt vinegar
1 apple

Cut the pork steak into medallions and flatten. Sauté mushrooms, onion and garlic. Seal the pork. It should cook in five minutes provided you have flattened it really thin. Add a touch of cream and paprika and serve on a bed of rice. See page 72 for how to cook the rice and page 13 for the red cabbage.

PORK MEDALLIONS
served with red cabbage
on a bed of rice

8 meringues
whipped cream

This is simply meringues (see page 42) topped with whipped cream.

MERINGUES CHANTILLY

PRAWNS IN GARLIC
delicious as a main course
or a starter

You would need to allow about 8 oz of cooked and peeled prawns for a main course, but here we are using less for a starter. Poach the prawns and top, tail and peel them. Toss them with the finely chopped garlic and a good knob of butter on a really hot pan. When the butter melts add a drop of brandy and a touch of lemon juice. For a really nice nutty flavour put the prawns in a ramekin dish under a hot grill for a few minutes. Sprinkle with chopped parsley and serve with lemon wedges and brown bread and butter.

8–12 oz (225–350g) cooked and peeled prawns
2 cloves of garlic
a little butter
a nip of brandy
some lemon juice
parsley
lemon wedges
brown bread
and butter

PORK CHOPS IN BREADCRUMBS
with red cabbage and
baked potatoes

A popular dish and easy to prepare.

Beat the chops thin between two sheets of greaseproof paper with a mallet. Dust lightly with flour and dip in egg wash before tossing in breadcrumbs. Make sure each chop is completely covered and shake off the excess, otherwise you'll have loose crumbs burning black on the pan as you cook. Heat the pan until very hot, add oil and butter and cook the chops two at a time.

It is important always to make sure that pork is well done as undercooked pork is very dangerous. There should be no trace of blood whatsoever. To ensure they are cooked through you can put the chops in a medium oven for an extra five minutes after frying. Don't put one on top of another as this makes them very greasy.

Serve with red cabbage and baked potatoes (see pages 13 and 66).

8 pork chops half-an-inch thick
a little flour
egg wash (2–3 eggs beaten with ¼ pint (150 ml) milk)
2 cups homemade breadcrumbs
a little oil
1 tablespoon butter

MANGO ICE CREAM

Peel the mango and slice all the flesh off the stone. If it is under-ripe you could stew it slightly, otherwise just mash it well. When cold blend with cream and whip until stiff, adding a little sugar to taste. Freeze.

1 mango
a carton of cream
sugar to taste

This is perfect for a Sunday dinner, although I'd get up in the night for bubble-and-squeak.

OYSTERS IN GARLIC BUTTER

MENU FOR 4

24 oysters
1 clove of garlic
a knob of butter
parsley and lemon to garnish

Try to get some seaweed over the oysters for taking them home. Do not open them too far in advance and keep in a cool place, but not in the fridge. To prepare, take the oysters out of their shells, taking care not to puncture them. Do not wash under the tap or you'll take away all the sea flavour. Dry and heat the shells in the oven.

Now all you do is heat the oysters in a hot pan with a knob of butter and the chopped garlic, then return to the heated shell and pour the garlic butter over the oysters. Then put a little piece of butter and more finely chopped garlic on top of each oyster and place under the grill until the butter becomes nutty. Garnish with a sprinkle of parsley and a wedge of lemon.

BAKED HAM
with bubble-and-squeak

2 lb (900g) ham (gammon off the bone)
1 teaspoon Colman's mustard
white breadcrumbs
a little white sugar

6 mashed potatoes
cooked cabbage

Boil the ham for twenty minutes to the pound and twenty minutes over, with mustard added to the water. When cooked leave to cool with the skin on. Cover the cooling ham with a wet cloth which has been submerged in the cooking water to keep the moisture in.

Next remove the skin and cover the ham with white homemade breadcrumbs and sugar and bake it in a hot oven until golden brown.

Serve with bubble-and-squeak, which is simply mashed potatoes with cooked cabbage through it, fried on a hot pan until brown and crisp. Lovely even for breakfast.

SHERRY TRIFLE

1 x 8 inch sponge cake half
a little raspberry jam
1 glass sherry
1 pt (600ml) custard
a little sugar
jubilee sauce (see page 98)
cream and cherries to decorate

I never use jelly in trifle. This gives it a texture like plaster of paris. I use sponge cake well crumbled with a little raspberry jam through it and moistened with sherry. Pour the custard over this and sprinkle a little sugar on top to prevent a skin forming and place it in the fridge to set. Finally pour the jubilee sauce over the trifle.

This dish is lovely presented in separate glasses decorated by dipping the rims in egg white or oil and coloured sugar. For a finishing touch use rosettes of cream and cherries.

A traditional Saturday supper in Dublin, coddle is just right served on its own. Long slow cooking is in order here, so there's no need to fret if there are latecomers to the meal, as it will come to no harm sitting on the stove.

DUBLIN CODDLE
terrific for a hangover

Coddle is Dublin's equivalent of the American's clam chowder or the French *soupe à l'oignon*. It is simple and inexpensive to make, but it is really delicious. I cooked it once at Bloomingdales in New York at an 'Ireland is a special place' exhibition and they went wild for it.

The bacon must be streaky, and the whole secret is that you don't put the onions, bacon and sausages in together, as that gives a very high grease content and no matter how you try to skim it off it will keep coming through. Instead I suggest you soak the bacon overnight and blanch the sausages in scalding water for a few minutes. Cut the pre-soaked bacon into strips and blanch it in the same way.

Cut the onions rather large and cook with four peeled potatoes in water. When these are nearly cooked add in the bacon and sausages. Cook the other potatoes separately and when the dish is ready to serve, peel and mash these and add to the coddle where they will absorb the remaining fat and act as a thickener. Don't be tempted to use instant potatoes or potatoes creamed with milk — just plain mashed potatoes.

Serve up sprinkled with parsley. I always think that any dish with a soupy consistency like coddle should be served in a bowl or soup plate so that the sauce can be scooped up — after all that's the best part.

8 streaky rashers of bacon
8 pork sausages
2 large onions
about 9 potatoes
some parsley

See page 89 for this recipe.

VEGETABLE SOUP

PORK FILLET WITH PAPRIKA AND SOUR CREAM

served with boiled long-grain rice

2 medium pork steaks
2 tablespoons butter
¼ cup finely chopped onion
1 tablespoon paprika
1 cup dry white wine
½ cup sour cream
chopped parsley

2 cups long-grain rice

This is easy and quick to prepare. An ideal party dish or delicious for lunch or supper.

Slice the pork.

Put the butter onto a very hot pan, add the onion and the pork pieces sprinkled with the paprika and sauté lightly. Pour in the white wine. Allow to simmer for five minutes.

Just before serving add in the sour cream and sprinkle with chopped parsley.

Serve with plain boiled rice (see page 72 for method).

RASPBERRIES IN MELON

with lemon wedges

½ lb (225g) raspberries
2 small Cantaloupe melons
1 lemon

Clean the raspberries with a dry cloth. Halve the melons and remove seeds. Fill the centres with the raspberries and decorate with lemon wedges.

You either like this dish or you don't, but it's full of goodness. It can take up to four hours in the cooking, so it's definitely not for folks in a hurry.

DISH FOR 4

TRIPE AND ONIONS
an old favourite

Get the butcher to slice up the tripe into pieces about two inches wide. This helps the cooking. Blanch the tripe in half-and-half milk and water with half a sliced onion to give the stock a nice flavour. Simmer until tender – this will take at least two hours.

Strain and save the stock. Now make a white sauce (see page 95) using the stock and sauté the onions in butter. Layer the tripe in a dish with the onions. Pour on the sauce and bake in a medium oven for half an hour.

2 lb (900g) tripe
4 large onions
some milk
a little flour
a little butter

FISH

This is one of those quick and simple menus. A lot of the preparation can be done beforehand.

MENU FOR 4

BAKED GRAPEFRUIT GRAND MARNIER

Cut the fruit in half. Remove the white centre and with a sharp knife free the fruit from the skin and make incisions in the segments.

Place on a baking dish and pour some Grand Marnier over them. (Brown sugar could be substituted for the liqueur if you wish.)

Cook in a medium oven for ten to fifteen minutes. If you have a couple of fresh grapes, green or black, seed them and place in the centre of the grapefruit before serving. Serve hot.

2 grapefruit
a nip of Grand Marnier

SEAFOOD SHISH KEBABS
on a bed of rice

Marinate the seafood in oil, fennel, garlic and wine for an hour or two and spear alternate pieces with the vegetables on a skewer. Bake them in the oven (medium) for twenty minutes. Serve on a bed of long-grain rice (see page 72).

8 shrimps
8 scallops
8 pieces of whitefish
1 cup oil
a sprig of fennel
1 clove of garlic
1 glass white wine
8 mushrooms
½ red pepper
4 small whole tomatoes

2 cups long-grain rice

MERINGUES AND ORANGE ICE CREAM

Meringues are the speciality of every mother with small babies. My wife Audrey always used up the leftover egg whites by making these prizewinners when the boys were small and consumers of egg yolks.

Whisk the whites until stiff and then whisk in half the sugar. When the mixture is stiff fold in the remainder of the sugar.

Make 3-inch meringues on lightly greased greaseproof paper. Meringues should always be proved in the airing cupboard or in a warm place for about an hour before being put in the oven. Then bake towards the bottom of a cool oven (gas mark ½–¾; 250°F; 125°C) until dry – about one to two hours.

To make the ice cream whip the cream until stiff and stir in half of the fresh orange juice – then gradually add in the rest. Blend in the sugar. Semi-freeze, then stir to break down the crystals. Add a nip of Cointreau and freeze again.

Serve in scoops with the meringues and garnish with angelica leaves.

3 egg whites
6 oz (175g) caster sugar

½ pint (300ml) double cream
½ pint (300ml) fresh orange juice
1 oz (25g) caster sugar
a nip of Cointreau
angelica to garnish

42

FRENCH ONION SOUP

This might be a bit heavy as a first course in warm weather, so you could serve it as a light lunch or supper dish on its own if you prefer. The recipe is on page 92.

GOUJONS OF SOLE
or plaice or even monkfish

1½ lb (700g) sole
flour for dusting
egg wash (2 eggs and ¼ pint (150ml) milk)
1 cup homemade breadcrumbs
lemon wedges to garnish

Served with baked leeks and boulangère potatoes this is a nice colourful menu and it makes good use of the oven, but it requires a bit of preparation.

Cut the fish into fingers, dust lightly in flour, dip in egg wash and breadcrumbs and deep fry in oil. Cook only a few at a time so that they don't get soggy. Drain on greaseproof paper before serving, garnished with lemon.

BAKED LEEKS

2 lb (900g) leeks
2 cloves of garlic
1 onion
6 tomatoes
½ cup white wine or stock
parsley
black pepper

This is another dish that is also delicious on its own. It can be fortified by adding mushrooms, peppers and celery, but this version is simple.

Blanch the leeks for five minutes. Drain and arrange in an oven-proof dish.

Sauté the finely chopped onion and garlic until soft and stir in the peeled and pulped tomatoes, wine and finely chopped parsley. Season with freshly ground black pepper.

Pour this sauce over the leeks and bake in a preheated oven gas mark 4 (350°F; 180°C) for forty five minutes.

BOULANGÈRE POTATOES
thinly sliced potatoes layered with finely sliced onions

8 or 9 potatoes
1 big onion
1 cup of water
a little butter

Peel and slice the potatoes and onions thinly and layer in a buttered ovenproof dish. Add the cup of water and butter well on top. Bake in the top of the oven until cooked and the top is crispy brown — about one hour.

CHOCOLATE SOUFFLÉ
can be varied to any flavour

This chocolate soufflé recipe can be varied to make a soufflé of any flavour, sweet or savoury. Soufflé is one of the most heartbreaking of all dishes, and in the past I've had my share of failures. After a lot of hard thought I've come up with this foolproof method, which I guarantee will have your soufflés coming up tops. You make a roux first and let it go cold, so leave yourself plenty of time for this.

Preheat the oven to gas mark 5 (375°F; 190°C).

First separate the eggs and put the whites in the fridge. Bring the milk to the boil. Meanwhile make the roux by melting the butter in a hot saucepan and gradually adding the flour, stirring in a figure-of-eight. Now pour in the milk until you have a stiff consistency – this is important to the success of your soufflé. Now allow this to go cold. When cold add the chocolate (or whatever flavouring you are using – cheese or Grand Marnier, for instance).

Mix three of the beaten egg yolks into the mixture to a creamy consistency. Then add the remaining beaten yolks. Whisk up the whites with the sugar (omit the sugar for a savoury soufflé of course) until stiff and fold into the mixture. The consistency should be very stiff.

Butter the soufflé dish. Fill it three-quarters full, leaving room for the soufflé to rise.

My tip is to stand the soufflé in a receptacle of boiling water on top of the stove for fifteen minutes before putting it in the oven, making sure there is enough water to cover the bottom part of the soufflé dish. Then cook it in the oven for a further fifteen minutes. This method ensures that instead of the soufflé flopping, you'll be able to cut through it like a madeira cake, for the simple reason that you have cooked the bottom beforehand. In the normal way the top of the soufflé rises beautifully, but collapses because the bottom is not cooked.

1 cup milk
3 oz (75g) sugar
3 oz (75g) flour
3 oz (75g) butter
6 large eggs
3 oz (75g) grated chocolate

MENU FOR 2 | See page 91 for this recipe.

2 sirloin steaks (1–1½lb; 450–700g)
6 oysters
a little butter
cayenne pepper

4–6 new potatoes
a cabbage heart

CARPET BAG STEAKS À LA BENT
with new potatoes and cabbage hearts

This exquisite and, I fear, expensive dish is simply sirloin steak stuffed with oysters. The combination of flavours is unbelievably good. It needs some attention, but is not really difficult.

Carefully remove the oysters from the shell. Using a sharp knife cut a pocket in the steaks and put three oysters in each. Season with cayenne. Skewer the pockets with wooden coctail sticks or sew them if you wish.

Now seal the steaks on a hot pan with the butter and place them in an ovenproof dish, pour the butter from the pan over them, and bake in a hot oven for ten to fifteen minutes, depending on how rare you like your steak.

Serve with boiled new potatoes (see page 14) and cabbage hearts (see page 26).

1 avocado
1 orange or 2 satsumas
lemon juice

AVOCADO DESSERT

This is an interesting change from avocado as a starter.

Halve the avocado and remove the stone. Squeeze a little lemon juice over the cut halves to keep the flesh from discolouring. Serve segments of peeled orange in the centre and squeeze more lemon juice on top.

A simple menu. The starter and dessert can be prepared well in advance and the main course can be cooking merrily in the oven giving you lots of time for your guests.

MENU FOR 4

EGG MAYONNAISE

See page 101 for this recipe.

BAKED HADDOCK STEAKS

Bake the steaks on a buttered dish in the oven (gas mark 5; 375°F; 190°C) with a knob of butter on top of each one for fifteen to twenty minutes.

4 haddock steaks
a little butter

STUFFED COURGETTES

Wash and trim the courgettes and split in half. Scoop out the flesh. Blanch the empty shells in boiling water for five minutes.

Sauté the finely chopped streaky rashers, garlic and onion. Chop the peeled tomatoes and the courgette flesh small and add them to the bacon mixture.

Season with ground black pepper and add the breadcrumbs. Press this mixture well into the courgette shells and bake in a hot oven for fifteen to twenty minutes.

4 courgettes
2 streaky rashers of bacon
1 clove of garlic
1 onion
2 tomatoes
1 tablespoon homemade breadcrumbs
black pepper
parsley to garnish

ANNA POTATOES

Line the thinly sliced potatoes in the bottom of a well-buttered ovenproof dish. Butter each layer well before adding the next layer of potatoes. Bake in the top of the oven for about an hour.

8–9 potatoes
butter

CHOCOLATE MOUSSE

Melt the chocolate over a bowl of boiling water. Separate the eggs, beat the yolks and stir into the melted chocolate, adding the orange juice, the melted butter and the Cointreau. Whisk the egg whites until stiff and fold well into the chocolate mixture. Pour into individual stem glasses and chill until set.

Decorate with whipped cream and flaked chocolate.

8 oz (225g) cooking chocolate
juice of 1 orange
4 eggs
a nip of Cointreau
2 oz (50g) butter
whipped cream
flaked chocolate

CRUNCHY GREEN SALAD

greens as available: lettuce, chicory, cabbage, Chinese leaves, endives, green peppers, avocados
lemon juice
French dressing

Crisp all the leaves in icy water and shred by hand, except cabbage if you are using it, which should be finely shredded with a knife or in a food processor. Slice the green peppers and the avocados (which should be sprinkled with a little lemon juice) and add to salad. Toss in French dressing just before serving.

FISH AND POTATO PIE

1½ lb (700g) cod
7 potatoes
a little flour
a little butter
a little milk
pepper
parsley
1 egg

Boil and mash the potatoes with a little milk, butter, pepper and parsley.

Poach the trimmed fish gently and keep the stock. Skin the fish and flake it. Now make a velouté (white sauce) with flour, butter, the fish stock and a little milk. Season with a little pepper and parsley and add the fish to the sauce.

Pour the mixture into an ovenproof dish and cover with the creamed potatoes. Coat with a beaten egg and cook in the top of a moderate oven until the potatoes are crispy and brown — about twenty minutes.

BAKED BANANAS
with rum and butter

4 bananas
2 oz (50g) brown sugar
a nip of rum
a little butter
whipped cream

Split the bananas and layer them in a well-buttered ovenproof dish with the brown sugar. Sprinkle the rum — or any liqueur you fancy — on top, dot with butter and bake in the centre of the oven for about fifteen minutes. Serve topped with cream.

There aren't many dishes that can be served in newspaper and still taste good. This recipe is suitable for fish fillets, fish steaks and whole small fish such as plaice, cod, haddock or whiting.

FISH AND CHIPS If you are using whole fish don't use the egg-and-breadcrumb or batter coating.

If using the flour coating, simply put the flour in a bag and toss the fish in it. If using the egg-and-breadcrumb coating dust the prepared fish in the flour, dip in egg wash, shake off excess egg wash and coat in breadcrumbs. Fry the coated fish in a heated pan with a little oil until cooked – about ten minutes, depending on size. Be careful when turning the fish – use a fish slice to avoid breaking it. Drain on greaseproof paper.

If you prefer to use a batter coating you should deep fry the fish.

Drain on greaseproof paper and garnish with lemon and parsley. Serve with chips (see page 80). If you haven't got a newspaper handy, plates will do just as well.

SUPPER DISH FOR 4

4 portions fish
to coat
seasoned flour
or
seasoned flour
egg wash (2 beaten eggs to milk)
1 cup breadcrumbs
or
fritter batter
to garnish
parsley
lemon
to serve on the side
chips for 4

½ lb (225g) chicken livers
½ lb (225g) streaky bacon
rashers
Worcester sauce

The devils make a super starter or a supper-time snack. They can be served individually with drinks and look well in kebabs.

Sauté the livers and wrap in the streaky rashers. Skewer, sprinkle with Worcester sauce and bake in a medium oven for fifteen to twenty minutes. Three or four on each skewer is enough for each person.

DEVILS ON HORSEBACK
chicken livers in streaky bacon

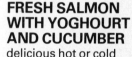

1 salmon
a bay leaf
a sprig of fennel
a knob of butter
a little white wine
a little malt vinegar

8–9 potatoes
or
potato salad

1 carton of yoghourt or sour cream
½ cucumber

This is perfect for a summertime special. Serve it hot with new potatoes (see page 14) or cold with potato salad (see page 102) as the mood suits you.

Scale the fish and wash it well in cold water. Remove the head. Taking the salmon off the bone is quite easy. All you have to do when making the incision is to ensure that you feel the knife rubbing against the bone. Place the two fillets in a receptacle and cover with water. Add a bay leaf, a sprig of fennel, a knob of butter and some white wine and vinegar. Cover with a sheet of greaseproof paper, which should be submerged so as not to burn while in oven. It's best to cook the fish in the oven — this way the fish is cooked from the inside. Cook in a preheated moderate oven for fifteen to twenty minutes.

Slice the cucumber thinly enough to be suspended in the yoghourt. Serve on the side with the salmon.

You will have lots of salmon left over for another meal.

FRESH SALMON WITH YOGHOURT AND CUCUMBER
delicious hot or cold

A selection of cheeses would make a nice ending to this summer meal.

CHEESE BOARD

FILLET OF SOLE AUX AMANDES
with salad and new potatoes

Nice as a fish course or a lunch dish.

Simply dust the sole in flour, place on an oiled tray, season and bake in hot oven for ten minutes. Take out the garnish with chipped almonds. Place under the grill for a few minutes before serving, with wedges of lemon and chopped parsley.

Toss the shredded salad greens in French dressing. Boil the potatoes.

DISH FOR 6

6 lemon sole
2 oz (50g) almonds
lemon wedges
chopped parsley

a head of lettuce
a head of Chinese leaves
watercress
1 green pepper
1 avocado
a head of chicory
French dressing

13–16 potatoes

MENU FOR 4 An expensive menu for a special occasion.

12–24 asparagus tips
Parmesan cheese or melted
butter or a little vinaigrette
dressing

ASPARAGUS TIPS

Cook the asparagus in three inches of boiling water with a little lemon juice and a knob of butter. Make sure all the tips are in the one direction – this helps when easing them out of the pot.

Cook for fifteen minutes covered with a sheet of greaseproof paper in the oven. Submerge the paper in the water so that it won't burn. Remove and drain.

Serve hot with parmesan cheese or melted butter or cold with vinaigrette dressing. You only eat the tips of course.

8 fillets of sole
4–8 oz (100–250g) cooked
lobster meat
2 oz (50g) flour
2 oz (50g) butter
½ cup of white wine
a drop of brandy
a little extra butter
3 oz (75g) grated Cheddar

FILLET OF SOLE WALESCA
lobster and sole in a white wine sauce

Dover sole would make this a splendid treat, but lemon sole is also fine for this dish which should not take any longer than five minutes to cook.

Place the sole in a flat dish with a little butter, a bay leaf, some fennel and seasoning and barely cover with water. Cover with a sheet of wet greaseproof paper and poach gently in the oven. It's important that the paper on top of the fish should be submerged in the water, otherwise it will burn as it dries.

Make a velouté (white sauce, see page 95) adding the sole stock and the white wine to the flour and butter roux. Stir in a figure-of-eight to a creamy consistency. Don't forget a little butter on top to stop a skin from forming.

Now slice the lobster meat into four scallops and toss in butter with a drop of brandy added. Take a deep dish and place each lobster scallop on top of a sole fillet and then another fillet on top of the lobster.

Now mask the sole pockets completly with the velouté and sprinkle on grated Cheddar cheese. Grill for a lovely golden glaze.

½ lb (200g) strawberries
4 scoops of ice cream
a nip of Cointreau
oz (100g) cooking chocolate

STRAWBERRY ROMANOFF
fresh strawberries,
Cointreau, ice cream and
chocolate sause

Place the strawberries in individual glasses. Top with ice cream and a drop of Cointreau and pour over the melted cooking chocolate for perfect results.

A straightforward menu. The lettuce soup can be served hot or cold and the syllabub prepared in advance.

MENU FOR 2

LETTUCE SOUP
with garlic croutons

Finely chop the onion and shred the lettuce, removing tough outer leaves if any. Sauté them in the butter until the onions are glassy. Make a roux by blending in the flour, stirring all the time in a figure-of-eight. Pour in the warmed milk, stirring all the time. Allow to cool, and put twice through a sieve.

Now gently beat the egg yolks with the cream, just enough to liquidise the yolks, and add to the soup. Return to heat, stirring as it thickens. Delicious hot or cold with garlic croutons. Make these by spreading garlic butter – a clove of garlic creamed in an ounce of butter – on bread, dicing and crisping in the oven.

2–3 lettuces
1 onion
1 oz (25g) butter
a little flour
1 pint (600ml) milk
black pepper
2 egg yolks
a carton of cream

OYSTERS EXCELSIOR
with duchesse potatoes
and baked courgettes

Remove the oysters carefully from their shells and poach them in a reduction of butter and white wine for two minutes. Meanwhile heat the shells in the oven. Now make a cheese sauce by adding the grated cheese to a basic white sauce (see page 95) and put the oysters, glazed in the sauce, back into the shells. Sprinkle with chopped hardboiled eggs and fresh white breadcrumbs and place under the grill until brown.

Duchesse potatoes are puréed with boiling milk, seasoning, butter and an egg yolk, piped into rosettes and browned in the oven.

24 oysters
2 oz (50g) butter
1 cup white wine
½ pint (300ml) milk
a little flour
2 oz (50g) grated cheese
1 cup homemade breadcrumbs
3 hardboiled eggs

3–4 potatoes

BAKED COURGETTES (ZUCCHINI)

Cut the courgettes – no need to peel – into thin slices and blanch in boiling water for a minute. Drain and make sure they are dry before arranging them in a well-buttered ovenproof dish. Sauté the finely chopped garlic in the butter and pour over the courgettes. Sprinkle with lemon juice and bake at gas mark 5 (375°F; 190°C) for twenty to thirty minutes. Garnish with parsley.

3–4 courgettes
1 clove of garlic
2 tablespoons butter
juice of ½ lemon
parsley

ORANGE SYLLABUB
simple and delicious

Beat the egg whites until stiff and fold in all the other ingredients except the orange rind, starting with the sugar. Pour into stem glasses and chill. Garnish with the grated rind and serve.

2 egg whites
4 oz (100g) caster sugar
juice and grated rind of 1 orange
½ pint (300ml) double cream

I look forward to this dish every year. The mackerel has to be caught fresh of course, carted home, heads trimmed and innards cleaned as soon as you've changed your wellingtons.

MUSTARD MACKEREL

MENU FOR 6

6–12 mackerel
Colman's mustard
lemon
parsley
butter
13 new potatoes

Mackerel is quite oily, but full of iron. Then of course there are those bones. But don't be put off. If you don't relish filleting, buy the mackerel filleted rather than miss out on the delicate flavour.

The more determined can take the fish in hand this way. Trim the heads and fins – I always leave the tails intact. Use a sharp pointy knife and split the fish open along the belly. Remove the entrails, and with a little rock or sea salt on your fingers, rub off the black inner skin. Next, turn the fish over flat with the shiny, striped side up, and press on the backbone. You'll feel the bones loosening under the pressure. Turn the fish over again and ease the backbone up. Pick out any small bones that are left. (This method applies for herrings as well.)

Boil the potatoes in salted water (see page 14). Coat the inside of the prepared mackerel with made-up mustard and place on a dish in the oven (gas mark 5; 375°F; 190°C) for ten to fifteen minutes until the tails turn up. If you like you can brown them under the grill for a minute. Garnish and serve with the new potatoes.

TOMATO SALAD

6 tomatoes
1 medium onion
oil and vinegar dressing

Serve a tomato salad on the side. Simply slice the tomatoes and onions finely and mix together. Serve with oil and vinegar dressing.

GOOSEBERRY FOOL

1 lb (450g) gooseberries
1 pint (600ml) custard
a small carton of cream
sugar to taste

Gooseberry fool goes very well after mackerel. Stew the gooseberries with sugar to taste and purée. Allow to cool and fold in custard and whipped cream. Chill.

CHICKEN LIVER PÂTÉ
a great standby

Sauté the finely chopped onion and garlic with one finely chopped streaky rasher. Add the chopped chicken livers, breadcrumbs and beaten egg. Mix well with the mace and salt and pepper as desired. Cook for a minute with the brandy.

Chicken liver pâté should be smooth so work it through a sieve or whizz it in a blender.

Line an oven proof dish with the rest of the rashers and smooth in the pâté. Bake in a medium oven for twenty minutes. Allow to go cold and pour the melted butter on top to preserve it. Serve in slices with triangles of toasted bread.

1 lb (450g) chicken livers
cooking oil
1 onion
1 clove of garlic
6 streaky rashers of bacon
1 cup homemade breadcrumbs
1 egg
seasoning
a pinch of powdered mace
a nip of brandy
2 oz (50g) butter

WHITE FISH PROVENÇALE
with rice

Colourful and economical dish.

Any white firm fish can be used, such as lemon sole, plaice, brill or turbot. Cut the fillet of fish into small pieces and toss in seasoned flour.

Then sauté the onion, garlic and peppers until soft but not brown. Add the floured fish and sauté with the vegetables for five minutes.

Finally add the tomato concasse (see page 72). Test that the fish is cooked. Serve with boiled rice (see page 72) either plain or brightened up with a little turmeric.

1 large fillet (about 2 lb; 1k) of white fish
½ onion
1 red pepper
½ green pepper
seasoned flour
4 tomato concasse
1 clove of garlic

2 cups long-grain rice
1 teaspoon turmeric (optional)

BANANAS JUBILEE

Make jubilee sauce as on page 98. Take the time to caramelise the butter and sugar – it makes all the difference. Then simply add the whole bananas. Don't allow them to go soggy.

4–6 bananas
jubilee sauce

This is a useful menu, ideal for winter or summer. The vichysoisse can be served hot or cold and the sole would make an excellent light lunch served with a salad.

VICHYSOISSE

The secret of this simple soup is a good stock, – chicken, potato or lamb.

Boil the well-washed, chopped leeks with the onion and diced potatoes in the stock and simmer until you have a creamy consistency. This will take about half an hour.

Vichysoisse should be smooth so strain carefully before adding the cream. Put a few knobs of butter on top to stop a skin forming. This soup is usually served cold. Place the soup in separate dishes and chill.

However, it is delicious hot too.

Sprinkle finely chopped spring onions and chives or parsley on top.

MENU FOR 6

2 pints (1 litre) chicken stock
3 large leeks
3 medium potatoes
1 large chopped onion
1 small carton of cream
a little butter
chives or parsley
spring onions (scallions)

FILLET OF SOLE CAPRICE
with banana and breadcrumbs

This is easy and economical and looks well.

Place half a split banana and a little butter on each fillet and put them on a tray in the oven preheated to gas mark 7 (425°F; 220°C). You must have the oven hot because it is the even heat which bakes the fish quickly.

Remove the sole from the oven, sprinkle with breadcrumbs and cayenne pepper and grill for a golden-brown effect. Garnish with wedges of lemon – no pips.

Serve with a salad (see page 13).

12 fillets of lemon sole
(about 4 oz (100g) each)
6 bananas
1 cup homemade
breadcrumbs
2 oz (50g) butter
cayenne pepper
lemon to garnish

PANCAKES JUBILEE
thin pancakes with ice cream and caramel sauce

Make the batter as on page 82. Heat the pan with oil and when it is really hot, throw off the excess and measure in the batter – I use a ladle – tilting to cover the circumference of the pan. Store the pancakes on top of each other.

pint (600ml) pancake batter
½ block (½ pint; 300ml) ice cream
a nip of Cointreau (optional)
1 tablespoon of whipped cream (optional)

jubilee sauce

continues overleaf

See page 98 for the sauce recipe.

Jubilee pancakes are stuffed with ice cream with the rich sauce poured over them, but for a special treat, add Cointreau in whipped cream to the ice cream – unbelievable.

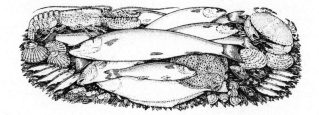

VEAL

CABBAGE HEARTS
stuffed with carrots in Madeira

Choose tender-leaf cabbage. Blanch the leaves in a small drop of boiling water in the bottom of a saucepan.

Dice the carrots very small and cook in very little water until really tender. Add a knob of butter and a drop or three of Madeira. You can use sherry if you have no Madeira.

Spoon the drained carrots onto the centre of the leaves, add a knob of butter and fold. Bake in a moderate oven oven for five to ten minutes.

leaves from the heart of 1–2 cabbages
4 carrots
a little butter
a little Madeira

ESCALOPES OF VEAL À LA CRÈME
with green noodles

Dust the veal with the flour. Sauté the chopped garlic, onion, mushrooms and butter on a hot pan. Add the veal – well flattened – and cook for two minutes.

Add the cream and cook for a further five minutes. Serve with green noodles, cooked for a few minutes in boiling water.

4 escalopes of veal
a little flour
4 oz (100g) butter
1 clove of garlic
1 onion
14 mushrooms
1 cup sour cream or double cream
1 lb (450g) green noodles

FRESH FRUIT SALAD IN HALF A PINEAPPLE WITH KIRSCH

Cut the four corners of the halved pineapples. Carefully remove the centre fruit and dice it. Return it with the other chopped fruits to the shell and sprinkle with kirsch.

2 pineapples
any other fruit – try fresh cherries and kiwifruit with pears
a sprinkling of kirsch

See page 91 for this recipe.

MINESTRONE SOUP

4 escalopes of veal
a little flour
egg wash (2 beaten eggs
with a little milk)
1 cup fresh homemade
breadcrumbs
1 hard-boiled egg
parsley to garnish
capers and anchovies

WIENER SCHNITZEL
with fresh broccoli and
baby soufflé potatoes

Dip the veal in flour, shake well, dip in egg wash and roll in breadcrumbs. Press the crumbs well in and make sure the veal is evenly coated.

Brown on a hot pan, turning just once.

Garnish each schnitzel with the hard-boiled egg – first separate the yolk from the white and chop very finely; then sprinkle first the yolk in a straight line and then the white, with a line of parsley in the centre.

Serve capers and anchovies separately and some melted butter on the side.

a head of broccoli
7–9 potatoes

Break the broccoli into florets and cook in bubbling water for ten minutes. Drain and serve with a knob of butter and seasoned to taste.

Peel and cut the potatoes into baby squares. Cook in warm – not boiling – water. When cooked, remove the spuds and bring the water to the boil. For the soufflé effect, plunge the cooked potatoes back into the boiling water and cook for one minute more. Strain and serve.

4 made pancakes
2 tablespoons raspberry jam

Make four pancakes (see page 82) and serve hot filled with heated raspberry jam.

**HOT JAM
PANCAKES**

59

Straightforward, easy to prepare, yet opulent enough for that special occasion.

OYSTERS KILPATRICK

Open the oysters turning each one back into its shell so that you don't lose any of the juice.

Cook the rashers until crispy, chop them up finely and sprinkle over the oysters with a little Worcester sauce for a piquant flavour.

Sprinkle with homemade breadcrumbs and brown under the grill.

12–24 oysters
3 streaky rashers of bacon
a little Worcester sauce
1 cup homemade breadcrumbs

VEAL HOLSTEIN

Season the veal and dip in flour, shake off excess and fry in butter on a hot pan. Serve with a fried egg on top. Put the fillets of anchovies and tiny pieces of smoked salmon on small square pieces of toast and decorate the dish with them. Garnish with lemon slices, lettuce leaves and capers.

4 escalopes of veal
seasoning
a little flour
a little butter
4 eggs
a few fillets of anchovies and small pieces of smoked salmon
bread for toasting
lemon slices, capers and lettuce leaves to garnish

STRAWBERRIES IN PORT

Marinate the strawberries in the port and serve.

¾–1lb (350–450g) strawberries
a wineglass of port

MENU FOR 4   A starter is not necessary with this fairly heavy main dish.

4 escalopes of veal
egg wash (3 eggs to ¼ pint
(150ml) milk)
paprika
4 slices white bread
4 slices Gruyère cheese
4 slices cooked ham
1 clove of garlic
½ pint (300ml) white sauce
(see page 95)
2 tomatoes
1 dessertspoon tomato
ketchup
½ teaspoon brown sugar

ESCALOPES OF VEAL BORDERLAISE

This tastes delicious. The veal is wafer-thin and the whole combination melts in the mouth.

Flatten the escalopes with a mallet between two sheets of greaseproof paper and season with paprika.

Dip the pieces in egg wash and then in the grated cheese. (You can use Cheddar instead of Gruyère.) Sauté on a hot pan with butter and a slice of ham for each escalope. At the same time fry a slice of bread, which has been soaked in egg wash, in garlic and butter. Place the ham on the bread and the veal on top and serve with tomato sauce on the side. To make the tomato sauce simply add the concassed and sieved tomatoes and the ketchup to the basic white sauce and sweeten with the sugar.

lettuce leaves
Chinese leaves
1 green pepper
1 red pepper
a few stuffed olives
2 shredded carrots
a little chopped onion
French dressing

MIXED VEGETABLE SALAD

This can be served on the side or after the main course. Simply follow the instructions on salad-making on page 13.
You shouldn't need a dessert if you have the salad as a refreshing second course, but you could serve cheese and crackers and fruit for very hungry guests.

LAMB

2 dozen oysters
½ cup white wine
a little butter
a little cream
a little grated Cheddar cheese

OYSTERS MORNAY
with white wine and cheese sauce

Delicious raw, oysters are rumoured to be a great aphrodisiac. They also contain enough protein, phosphorus and iodine for a human being's requirements. Because they are so expensive this dish would be best as a starter or fish course.

Remove the oysters from the shell, taking care not to puncture them. Heat the unwashed shells in the oven.

Reduce the wine with a knob of butter on a hot pan and cook the oysters in this for two minutes. Add a little cream and some grated cheese. Replace in the shells and sprinkle some more cheese on top.

Put them under the grill to glaze for a minute before serving.

a rack of lamb
1 cup cold coffee
1 cup redcurrant jelly

4 cabbage hearts
a little butter

RACK OF LAMB
cooked with coffee and redcurrent jelly

This combination is unusual and the resulting flavour unbelievably good.

Strip all the fat and then the muscle off the meat, cover it completely in redcurrant jelly and pour the cold coffee over it. Bake in a very hot oven (at least gas mark 7; 425°F; 220°C), the hotter the better.

Cook the cabbage hearts for two minutes in boiling water, just enough to cover the bottom of the saucepan. Strain. Add a knob of butter and serve.

6–7 potatoes
1 large onion

LYONNAISE POTATOES

Peel and slice the potatoes and sauté, using a little oil on a hot pan, with the thinly sliced onions.

Layer them on a dish, making sure the onions are underneath, and grill until nicely browned.

1 lb (450g) blueberries
a little lemon juice
a little caster sugar

BLUEBERRIES

Wash and trim the fruit, soak in a little lemon juice and toss in caster sugar.

IRISH STEW   Contrary to what people think Irish stew is not just meat and potatoes floating around in a pot of water. There is a lot of work for best results.

Give yourself time for this dish. In fact it is better to blanch the meat the day before. The next day you will find that all the fat has settled on the top and can be easily skimmed off. Keep the stock.

Cut away almost all the fat from the top of the ribs and pull away the thin layer of meat and fat on top of each rack. This layer is connected by a thin membrane. Cut away all the meat from the tops of the spare ribs, leaving the loin meat intact. Discard the meat trimmings.

Cut between the ribs, separating them into chops. Set aside.

Peel the potatoes, dropping them into cold water to prevent discoloration. Now cut three of them crosswise in half and cut the remaining two into quarters. Leave in cold water until ready to use.

Run the lamb under cold water until the water runs clear. Drain well. Arrange the chops neatly over the bottom of the casserole and add the cold water. Add salt and pepper to taste and bring to the boil.

The moment the liquid comes to the boil, strain the cooking liquid and set it aside.

Run the chops under cold water to chill well. Drain. Then return them to a clean casserole or kettle and cover with the onions cut into wedges.

Drain the halved and quartered potatoes and arrange the halved potatoes around the sides of the casserole over the chops. Skim off all the scum and fat from the reserved liquid and add the liquid to the chops in the casserole.

Cover the contents of the casserole with several layers of wax paper and bring to the boil. The paper must touch the top of the stew. Cook about half an hour.

Meanwhile put the quartered potatoes into a saucepan with cold water to cover and bring to the boil. Cook about twenty minutes

a rack of lamb (about 1¼ lb (500–600g) boned weight)
2 or 3 large onions
5 medium to large potatoes
5½ cups cold water
seasoning

over a high heat until the potatoes are almost falling apart and most of the liquid has evaporated. Add the remaining potato-water to the stew and mash the boiled potatoes. Add this mash, stirring it gently into the stew. Cover the top of the stew once more with wax paper and continue cooking over a very gentle heat for ten minutes.

This stew has a soupy consistency and should be served in soup bowls with a knife, fork and soup spoon.

A colourful menu, the starter and dessert are easy to prepare while the lamb and potatoes bake in the oven.

HARD BOILED EGGS STUFFED WITH CAVIAR
served on hot buttered toast

Hardboil the eggs, shell and halve. Remove the yolks and cream with mayonnaise. Return to eggwhite centre and top with caviar.

Serve on hot buttered toast which should be made at the last moment. Don't forget to butter both sides before toasting.

6 hardboiled eggs
a small pot of red caviar
toast and butter

CROWN OF LAMB
served with French beans, young carrots and baked potatoes

The butcher will prepare the crown for you. Allow at least six cutlets on each side. Bake it in the centre of the oven gas mark 4 (350°F; 180°C) with the bone facing out and the meat facing in. Place squares of bread to prevent the bone ends from burning. Allow thirty minutes to the pound.

Serve with cutlet frills (instead of the bread squares) on the bone ends for a more glamourous effect.

Serve with mint sauce (see page 68).

Cook the French beans and young carrots in very little water with a drop of Madeira (sherry will do) and a knob of butter to give them a sheen.

2 pieces best end of neck of lamb
mint sauce
1 lb (450g) French beans
1 lb (450g) young carrots
a drop of Madeira or sherry
a little butter

BAKED POTATOES WITH CHIVES

Bake the potatoes on a tray of salt. Remove from the oven, cut off the tops and scoop out the insides. Cream them with butter, pepper and finely chopped chives. Replace in the potato shells.

12–14 potatoes
a little butter
pepper

STRAWBERRY SURPRISE

Purée or grate the strawberries with Cointreau and fold into the whipped cream.

1 lb (450g) strawberries
a carton of cream
a nip of Cointreau

MENU FOR 1

2–3 pieces of lamb's liver a little flour	Good for lunch – quick and easy. Don't have the pieces too thick. Dust very lightly in flour and toss on a hot pan. (A cold pan leaves it soft and gooey.) The liver cooks in just a few minutes. Ideal to serve with ratatouille (see page 68) and fluffy new potatoes (see page 14).	**LAMB'S LIVER**
¼ lb (100g) strawberries a little caster sugar a small carton of cream	Sprinkle the strawberries with caster sugar and serve whipped cream on the side.	**FRESH STRAWBERRIES** and cream

DISH FOR 6

12 lamb kidneys (or 6 pork)
12 sausages
a little butter
1 onion
1 clove of garlic
a little flour
6 tomatoes concassed
½ pint (300 ml) beef stock
 	
2 cups long-grain rice
	This appetising dish is simply fried kidneys and sausages served on a bed of rice with a brown sauce. Suitable for large numbers.
	
	Blanch the kidneys (see note on page 84). Cut into dice, removing all the sinew. Sauté on a hot pan. Remove from pan.
	    Now fry the sausages in the same pan. When cooked cut them into small pieces.
	    To make the sauce throw off any excess fat from the pan and return it to the stove. Watch the residue from the kidneys and sausages bubble up – all the goodness is in there. Add a knob of butter, a little chopped onion and garlic and a touch of flour to make a roux, stirring all the time in a figure-of-eight.
	    Next add the tomato concasse and the beef stock. Finally add the kidneys and sausages; if you do not wish to serve the dish immediately put a few knobs of butter on top to stop a skin forming. Serve on a bed of rice (see page 72).
		KIDNEY TURBEGO
		on a bed of rice

A good combination of flavours and quite delicious. The rack of lamb cooks very quickly once the fat is trimmed off. Hot avocados are interesting and easy to do.

HOT AVOCADO CHEESE

Halve the avocados and remove the stones. A squeeze of lemon juice will prevent them from discolouring. Fill the hole with grated Cheddar and bake in a hot oven for a few minutes, until the cheese melts.

2 avocados
a little lemon juice
2 oz (50g) Cheddar cheese

RACK OF LAMB
with mint sauce

Strip all the fat off the lamb and then the muscle. Bake in a hot oven — gas mark 7 (425°F; 220°C) — in fact the hotter the better. This takes only about twenty minutes.

a rack of lamb

FRESH MINT SAUCE

This is easy. Sprinkle the mint with sugar so it doesn't stick to the knife and chop it finely. Add a drop of malt vinegar and a dash of boiling water — and there you are.

a handful of fresh mint leaves
a little sugar
a dash of malt vinegar
a dash of boiling water

CROQUETTE POTATOES

There is only one way to do these properly.

Boil the spuds and make sure all the moisture is drained off. Season as desired and mash well, adding the egg yolk.

Now dust your hands with flour and knead the mash. The heat of your hands binds the croquettes. Fashion portions into barrels, dust them in flour and then in egg wash. Now roll in white breadcrumbs.

Keep the barrels apart as they are inclined to throw off condensation and you don't want soggy croquettes.

Deep fry in hot oil, one or two at a time.

8 potatoes
2 egg yolks
a little flour
egg wash (2 beaten eggs and a little milk)
1 cup white breadcrumbs

RATATOUILLE

Chop all the vegetables up finely and concasse the tomatoes. I never use tinned tomatoes as they are too limp and go into juice. Fresh tomatoes act as a thickener.

I normally start with a very hot pan and sauté off the garlic, onions, celery and courgettes (zucchini) for a few minutes. Then I add the peppers followed by the tomatoes.

Cook for just a few minutes longer. Vegetables should always be served fresh and crunchy, not boiled to a pulp.

It would be a good idea to serve the ratatouille on a side plate so that it won't make the croquettes soggy.

1 clove of garlic
1 onion
3 sticks of celery
2 courgettes
1 red pepper
1 green pepper
4 tomatoes

12 egg yolks
6 teaspoons sugar
1 glass Marsala
1 egg white
a little coloured sugar

ZABAGLIONE

This takes a little care to ensure the eggs don't curdle. Beat the egg yolks, sugar and Marsala over a low heat until they thicken. It's best to do this using a bain marie – that is over a pan of hot water – but if you prefer to do it in a single pot you should add a little water to the egg mixture to prevent the eggs from curdling.

Now pour the custard into goblets whose rims have been dipped in beaten egg white and then in coloured sugar. Serve warm.

PINEAPPLE AND PRAWNS

Pineapple and prawns make a refreshing combination to start this simple summertime meal. Scoop out and dice the flesh of half the pineapple. Fold through some mayonnaise and add the cooked prawns and a drop of rum.

½ pineapple
mayonnaise
10–12 prawns
a nip of rum

LAMB CUTLETS
with mushrooms and spicy rice

Lamb cutlets are perfect for summer weather. The quick and easy method is to take off all the fat until you have the 'eye' of the cutlet. It should look like a lollipop. Flatten it if the meat is too thick as if it is it will be underdone and the breadcrumbs will become soggy.

Dust the cutlet in flour, shake off the excess, dip in egg wash and roll in breadcrumbs. Pat carefully to ensure that the meat is completely covered.

Seal on a hot pan with a little oil and cook for a few minutes. Drain on greaseproof paper. Complete the cooking in the oven gas mark 4 (350°F; 180°C) to ensure that the cutlets are cooked right through. The breadcrumbs will come up crisp and appetising.

2 lamb cutlets
flour
2 eggs
little milk
1 cup breadcrumbs

SPICY RICE

Cook the rice and add a teaspoon of curry powder to it. Sauté the sliced mushrooms for one minute and fold them through the rice. This can be served hot or cold. Colour with turmeric, and add some green and red peppers or avocado pear for variety.

1 cup long-grain rice
2 oz (50g) mushrooms
1 teaspoon curry powder
turmeric, red and green
pepper and avocado pear
(optional)

CRISP GREEN SALAD

A crisp green salad (see page 47) can be served on the side or as a final course.

CURRY

Contrary to what a lot of people might think, curry is best served immediately it is cooked rather than left for hours on the stove simmering. The point to remember is that anything that has herbs or spices in it should be cooked and served immediately.

Although curry is traditionally a 'hot' dish, tabasco or cayenne pepper should never be used. A truly hot curry has nothing to do with temperature — you'll find that out after it has reached the bottom of your throat. The real test is how soon you start to sweat — the ladies perspire of course.

Curry is always best served in bowls rather than on a flat plate for more comfortable eating.

CONDIMENT TRAY These are what make the dish. The condiments should be laid out on a long tray with a spoon or fork for each one.

ROASTED CURRANTS Toss in the pan for a few minutes with a knob of butter.

CHOPPED APPLES AND BANANAS Always put a drop of lemon juice over the bananas and apples to retain the colour.

CONCASSED TOMATOES Scald the tomatoes whole in boiling water. Remove the skins and seeds and chop roughly.

TOASTED COCONUT Simply toast desiccated coconut in the oven.

POPPADUMS AND CHUTNEY No curry would be complete without them. Bought in delicatessens, poppadums should be cooked in very hot oil and they will puff up light and crispy.

They should be crunched and folded through the dish rather than eaten on the side. Try it and taste the difference.

BOMBAY DUCK A dried fish bought in delicatessens.

BOILED RICE Two cups of rice to five cups of water will give four servings. The water must be boiling before you add the rice. Add a slice of lemon (no pips) to keep the grains white, or a teaspoon of turmeric if you want bright yellow rice. Allow the water to boil up again and then boil it off the rice.

The secret of getting the starch out is to place a saucer upside down in a colander, add the cooked rice and allow cold water to seep through. The saucer prevents the holes from clogging up with rice.

Reheat the rice by pouring fresh boiling water over it and when drained and dry, add a knob of butter.

A to Z of curries

Using the basic method described on page 75 you can make various curries using prawns, chicken, lamb or beef. Here are a few more varieties you might like to try.

AGRA Artichokes
BENGAL Beef and button onions
BOMBAY Beef and diced potatoes
BORNEO Chicken, kidney and bacon
CANTON Chicken and ginger
COPTIC Meatballs, pimento and onions
COUNTRY CAPTAIN Game and fruit
DRY Minced corned beef and fried onions
EAST INDIA Lamb and apples
IRELAND Sweetbreads and button onions
JOHORE Veal, eggplant (aubergine) and apples
KOFTA Small cakes of minced beef

Beef with apples and ginger **LORD CLIVE**
Mutton and carrots **MALAY**
Pork, apples, tomatoes **MYSORE** and green chillies
Beef and turnips **NEPAL**
Mutton and gherkins **PENANG**
Quennelles of veal **QUORMA**
Mutton and pineapple **SINGAPORE**
Beef, onions and cucumber **SINGHALESE**
Frogs' legs **SOURABAYA**
Lamb, peas and **SUMATRA** eggplant (aubergine)
Beef strips soaked in vinegar **VINDALOO**
Sheep's heads with peas **ZANZIBAR**

PRAWN CURRY Curry is suitable when catering for large numbers.

Ask the delicatessen to make up the spices for you.

Prepare the prawns – top and tail and remove the shells. Make the curry in the usual way – see page 75. If you are using whole coconuts grate the flesh and use the milk as stock.

see page 75

PARTY DISH FOR 40

10 lb (4–5kg) prawns
20–30 onions
20–30 gloves of garlic
butter
12 oz (350g) coriander seed
1 oz (25g) chillies
2 oz (50g) turmeric
1/8 oz (3g) fenugreek
1/4 oz (5g) cummin seed
1 oz (25g) green ginger
1 lb (450g) dried coconut or
two whole coconuts

EGG CURRY This is made in the same way.

PARTY DISH FOR 40

40 hard-boiled eggs
10 onions
5 oz (130g) coriander
2 oz (50g) turmeric
1/4 oz (5g) cummin seed
1/8 oz (3g) pepper corns
1/4 oz (5g) chillies
1/2 oz (10g) fresh ginger
5 cloves of garlic
2 oz (50g) tamarind (pulped)
5 cups coconut
1 oz (25g) ground rice

MULLIGATAWNY SOUP

1½ pints (800ml) beef stock
1 onion
2 carrots
1 stick of celery
4 tomatoes
½ green pepper
½ red pepper
1 oz (25g) flour or cornflour
1 oz (25g) butter
1 tablespoon curry powder
1 oz (25g) cooked rice

Mulligatawny soup is made exactly as a vegetable soup (see page 89), spiced with some curry powder. When making your roux, simply add a tablespoon of curry powder. This gives it that strong yellow colour. Use one ounce of cooked rice to garnish and serve.

CHICKEN CURRY
with rice

1 onion
1 clove of garlic
1 large chicken
a little butter or margarine
2 tablespoons curry powder
1 tablespoon turmeric
1 carton of cream
2 cartons of natural yoghourt

2 cups long-grain rice
1 teaspoon of turmeric

Gently sauté the chopped onion and garlic in butter. (Traditionally ghee is used, but it is not readily available in Ireland.)

Add in the sliced chicken. You can use cooked chicken if you wish but raw chicken, especially if it is chopped finely, takes only a matter of minutes to cook.

When the ingredients are cooked add the curry powder and the turmeric. The strength of the curry powder to use is up to you but it is better to go easy with spices. Ask your delicatessen to mix them for you, if you are unsure. I use two tablespoons of curry powder with a tablespoon of turmeric for a medium hot curry. (Saffron is best, of course, but so expensive nowadays that it is beyond the pocket of the home cook and turmeric works almost as well.)

The spices take about ten minutes to cook and the curry is completed by adding cream or yoghourt or both to break down the consistency. A mixture of the two is best as yoghourt on its own is inclined to curdle when heated.

Serve the curry on a bed of yellow rice made by adding a teaspoon of turmeric to the boiling water.

MANDARINS

8–12 mandarins

Serve whole cold mandarins as a refreshing dessert after curry.

You wouldn't need a starter with this menu. Try it as a lunch or supper. The combination is just right.

MENU FOR 4

KEBAB CURRY Blend the spices well in with the minced meat. (Don't use leftovers.) Fashion into meat balls – six per person – and brown on the pan. Finish cooking in the oven – about twenty minutes in a preheated medium oven.

    Serve on a bed of fluffy white rice. Do not skewer the meat balls or they will break up.

1¾ lb (900g) freshly minced beef
2 tablespoons curry powder
2 cups long-grain rice

ORANGE SALAD You'll find this refreshing. Peel and slice the oranges. Remove pips and chill.

    Serve on lettuce heart leaves and dress with sour cream (see page 98).

lettuce heart leaves
4 oranges
sour cream

A cheap dish, ideal for large numbers. There is a lot of meat on chicken wings.

DISH FOR 6

3 lb (1.5kg) chicken winglets
3 onions
2 cloves of garlic
2 tablespoons curry powder
1 tablespoon turmeric
2 cartons yoghourt
1 carton of cream
3 cups long-grained rice

Boil the winglets until tender and keep the stock. Make the curry as on page 75, but break down the consistency with a little of the winglet stock, yoghourt and cream.
  Serve with rice, cooked as on page 72.

CHICKEN WINGLET CURRY

1 cucumber
6 tomatoes
lemon or orange juice

Slice the cucumber thinly, removing the skin if it is tough. Segment the tomatoes and dress with lemon juice for a piquant taste. Orange juice is an interesting alternative.

CUCUMBER AND TOMATO SALAD

CHILDREN

Cooking for children causes quite a few headaches. Getting them to eat what we think they should have is quite a problem, especially if they happen to sit beside a child at school who has a lunch-pack full of biscuits, crisps and fizzy drinks.

Talk to children about food and encourage them to grow vegetables in their own patch, even if it is only an onion in a window box. Children will always eat when they are hungry, so nothing in between meals encourages them and leaves them with an appetite, but the biggest success story of all is to let them cook. It is no secret that children will eat anything they cook themselves. It may be a bit of a bother to have them under your feet in the kitchen but it works and is one way of educating young taste buds.

Start with their favourites like hamburgers and fish fingers, and go on from there. Stick to savoury foods in the beginning so that this little 'game' doesn't become identified with sweet treats. And most of all think small. Two little hamburgers, meat balls or fish cakes will be demolished much faster than one big sturdy helping.

CHEESE AND TOMATO PIE

per person
1 egg
a little milk
2 slices of bread
1 tomato
a little grated cheese

Any little person who can read can make this without any adult help.

Beat up an egg with a little milk in a flat dish – a soup dish, for instance.

Rub a little margarine around a little dish. A dessert dish is fine for one person, but make sure it is one that will be all right in the oven.

Take the crusts off the bread and dip it in the egg-and-milk mixture. Now put a layer of bread in the bottom of the greased dish, and put a layer of sliced tomato and grated cheese on top of that. Then put another layer of dipped bread, and so on until the dish is full, ending with a cheese and tomato layer. In a small dish two layers will probably be enough.

Now pour the rest of the eggy mixture on top and put your dish in a hot oven (gas mark 7; 425°F; 220°C) for ten minutes. It will rise up like a soufflé.

You could make this just for yourself, but if you make an individual dish for each person in the family they are sure to love it.

QUEEN OF PUDDING

per person
1 piece of sponge cake
a little raspberry jam
1 egg
1 dessertspoon of sugar

While you have the oven on you could have a bash at this too. You can make individual dishes if you like, or put enough for everybody into one bigger dish. Grease the dish or dishes with margarine as you did for the pie and again make sure it is ovenproof.

Now crumble some sponge into the dish and stir in a little raspberry jam. Make an egg-and-milk mixture, but this time use only the egg yolk. Beat up the white separately with the sugar into meringue and pile this on top.

You can bake this at the same heat as your pie, but you should get a grown-up to put it in a tray of hot water for you.

Leave it in the oven until the meringue is nice and brown.

HAMBURGERS AND CHIPS

Sauté the finely chopped onion and soak the bread – with the crusts removed – in the milk. Drain off the milk and mix the bread through the mince with the sautéed onion. The soaked bread makes a much softer hamburger – one of the complaints children often have about homemade hamburgers is that they are too hard, and this is the answer.

Finally add a little tomato ketchup and I guarantee the children will go mad for them. You can let them shape their own burgers or pat them or do whatever they like to put their mark on them, which is their seal of approval.

These hamburgers will cook in minutes on a hot pan.

We can't get away from chips – children just love them. I don't recommend that children should be allowed to cook chips, as we all know that most kitchen fires start with chip-pans full of hot oil. But they can learn to treat this receptacle with respect by watching adults being careful.

The potatoes should be peeled, washed and dried carefully. This is where the kids come in – watch those little hands drying them to perfection.

Now cut the spuds into chips and deep fry in hot oil. When cooked toss the chips on greaseproof paper to get rid of excess fat before serving.

¾ lb (350g) freshly minced round steak
6–8 slices of bread
a little milk
½ onion
a little tomato ketchup

BREAD-AND-BUTTER PUDDING

Make an egg wash with the eggs and milk and dip the slices of bread – with the crusts removed – in it. Grease an ovenproof dish and put a layer of the dipped bread on the bottom. Sprinkle some currants on top and put another layer of bread on top of that. Continue with alternate layers of bread and currants until the dish is full, ending with a layer of bread. Pour the rest of the egg wash over the lot and sprinkle the dish with nutmeg. Bake in a preheated oven (gas mark 5; 375°F; 190°C) until golden brown.

8 slices of bread
3 eggs
a little milk
a handful or two of currants
a little nutmeg

SPAGHETTI BOLOGNESE

1 onion
¾ lb (350g) mince
a little oil
a little flour
a little tomato ketchup

6 oz (175g) spaghetti

Sauté the finely chopped onion with the mince until it is nicely browned right through. Don't add any water – just let it cook in its own juice.

Meanwhile cook the spaghetti in a large pot of boiling water with a little drop of oil to keep the strands of pasta separate. Don't overcook the spaghetti – leave a little 'bone' in it, or serve it 'al dente' as the Italians say. Children prefer it this way, as they don't like to eat things that feel slimy.

Now add a touch of flour to the meat sauce, flavour with a little ketchup, and pour this over the spaghetti. You'll find the meat sticks to the pasta, which is how it should be.

BANANA SPLITS

4 bananas
ice cream

A simple and popular dessert – simply split bananas topped with ice cream.

TOAD IN THE HOLE

12 sausages
1 pint (600ml) batter

This sausage dish with Yorkshire pudding is delicious and a favourite with children.

First cook the sausages in the oven. Then make a batter as described on page 82. It should be quite thin, just thick enough to mask the spoon.

Put the cooked sausages in an ovenproof greased dish. Pour the batter over them and cook in a medium oven (gas mark 5; 375°F; 190°C) until the batter has risen and has browned. Don't open the door to have a look or the batter will flop. I can assure you it will be ready in eactly ten minutes.

This can also be prepared in individual dishes, using three sausages per person.

APPLE TART AND ICE CREAM

Kids will generally eat anything so long as there's ice cream with it.

PANCAKE BATTER

Children love pancakes and there are several ideas for serving them throughout this book. They are also delicious just with lemon juice and caster sugar. Here is the batter recipe.

Try and find the time to make the batter a few hours in advance. This gives it a chance to ferment and will result in lighter pancakes.

An important rule to remember is that the eggs and part of the milk are beaten together first and *then* the flour is added exactly as if you are making a dough. Break the consistency down with the remainder of the milk. Pass through a strainer to guarantee a no-lump batter, which should have the consistency to mask the spoon as it is dropped off.

8 oz (225g) plain flour
a pinch of salt
1 pint (570ml) milk
2 eggs

FRITTER BATTER

Fruit fritters are another favourite. Use this batter recipe, dip slices of whatever fruit you have to hand in it and deep fry for a delicious dessert. Fritter batter is made in the same way as pancake batter, but it should be thicker. Add extra flour if you think it is too thin.

Always drain off the fritters before putting them in hot oil to ensure that they are light and not a ball of dough.

8 oz (225g) plain flour
a pinch of salt
½ pint (300ml) milk
2 eggs

GOURMET BREAKFAST OR BRUNCH

Nowadays people are inclined to run out the door in the mornings on a cup of tea instead of having a proper breakfast. This is not very wise and anybody who has any respect for their insides should eat a substantial breakfast.

Children especially need a good breakfast. A recent survey in Britain showed that a lot of little people eat very little in the morning, making them less alert and receptive to their work.

After all, breakfast is literally breaking the night fast and the custom of eating a roll or drinking a cup of coffee is relatively new in this country. It reflects an urban lifestyle, whereby people top up on tea-breaks and lunches, and is not rooted in the peasant community. In the Soviet Union, in the tourist hotels, breakfast consists of sausages, sauerkraut, blinis – which are Russian pancakes – drinking yoghourt, black bread, cheese, apricots and even beer – a stiff breakfast suitable for the worker operating in a climate of fourteen degrees below zero.

The traditional Irish brekky consists of bacon, eggs, brown cake and even fried potatoes. Part of the old concept, which makes sense, was to use up leftovers from the night before.

Porridge, made the night before, was a great standby. Eaten with cream and a glass of buttermilk it is excellent, and to my mind better than the popular cereals of today. Supplemented with a boiled egg, strips of bacon or black pudding, there is nothing better to put roses on your cheeks.

This gourmet menu was prepared as a treat for those who have forgotten what a good breakfast is like.

MIXED GRILL Although this is a 'grill' you can cook most of it in the oven.

LIVER Liver – lamb's is best – should be cut in scallops, not too thin and not too thick, and dusted very lightly in flour and fried gently. It always surprises people to hear that liver should be eaten underdone, but it should; also kidneys. Lightly cooked, all the goodness remains and they are easier to digest. Always make sure liver and kidneys are fresh. Watch out for holes in the liver. They make it taste bitter and tough.

KIDNEYS Blanch the kidneys – again lambs' are best. Remove skin and cut in half. Drop them into a pan of cold water and remove them just before it comes to the boil. This acts as a cleanser. You'll see all the residue coming to the top of the water. Then wash kidneys under a cold tap. Finish cooking them in a hot pan with a knob of butter.

BACON Bacon I always cook in the oven. The even heat gives a lovely crispy rasher.

SAUSAGES Blanch the sausages in hot water and cook in the oven – they turn out delicious, crispy and brown.

FIELD MUSHROOMS Cook flat mushrooms on a tray with a knob of butter and some salt and pepper in the oven for five minutes.

TOMATOES Tomatoes I always leave whole. Cut a cross on top and sprinkle with grated Cheddar cheese. This way they retain the juices and goodness when being cooked in the oven, or if you prefer browned under the grill.

CUTLET Grill the cutlet.

MÁIRE ÁINE POTATOES Some people like these to complete the dish. Use cold potatoes that were cooked in their jackets. Peel and slice them neatly and cook them on a hot pan with a little fat until golden brown. Sprinkle with salt if desired and serve with chopped parsley.

per person
1 sausage
1 rasher of bacon
½ pork kidney or 1 lamb's kidney
1 scallop of lamb's liver
1 lamb cutlet
1 flat field mushroom
1 tomato
1 cooked potato (optional)

84

A snipe of champagne will do. Serve with the juice of freshly squeezed oranges. Two measures of fruit juice to one of champers.

FRESH ORANGE JUICE AND CHAMPAGNE

The recipe for baked grapefruit Grand Marnier is on page 42. It is said that grapefruit burns excess fat in food and cleanses out the mouth for the rest of the day. Don't believe a word of it, but it is a refreshing starter.

BAKED GRAPEFRUIT GRAND MARNIER

Beat the eggs but don't add milk or water it will just break down the strength of the eggs.

Heat the pan, add a knob of butter and follow immediately with the eggs. Using a wooden spoon, make a figure-of-eight around the pan and in a few minutes you'll have beautiful lightly scrambled eggs.

Cut the smoked salmon into fine strips and sprinkle on top. Serve on toast.

SMOKED SALMON SCRAMBLED EGGS

An alternative to this is a patience omelette or poached eggs Valentino.

Omelettes should always be eaten on their own, I think, and of course each omelette will be cooked separately too, so people will have to be patient for their patience omelette.

Always have a special omelette pan – it makes all the difference. Otherwise the albumen in the eggs will stick to pans used for other cooking. Fillings for omelettes – mushrooms, ham etc – should be cooked separately.

Poach and flake the haddock.

Heat the pan well, until the oil goes blue. Throw off excess oil. Beat the eggs by hand at the last minute. Now put a knob of butter on the pan – do not allow it to clarify – and immediately add the eggs. Stir the eggs in a figure-of-eight to cover the surface of the pan

PATIENCE OMELETTE
with flaked haddock and cheese

er person
–3 eggs
knob of butter or a little oil
oz (75g) haddock
tablespoons Hollandaise
auce (see page 97)
sprinkling of parmesan

and cook the omelette. To shape the omelette, tilt the pan and tap the handle – you'll find the omelette will slip into shape.

Now turn your omelette onto a hot plate and put the hot haddock – heated with a knob of butter if necessary – onto the centre of the omelette. Pour the Hollandaise sauce over the lot, sprinkle with parmesan and glaze under the grill for two minutes.

POACHED EGGS VALENTINO

There is only one secret for perfect poached eggs – have the water boiling in the saucepan. This way the egg will not drop to the bottom and stick to the pot.

Add a drop of lemon or vinegar to the boiling water. Just watch it – in a few minutes the white will wrap around the yolk as it rises to the top.

Poached eggs can be prepared in advance and reheated at the last moment when the rest of the breakfast is ready to serve. Simply remove the eggs and place them in a receptacle of cold water. Then, when you are ready, place them once again into boiling water for a few seconds and you will still have a soft poached egg. Try it.

Serve on toast.

SOUPS

As far as I am concerned you can't beat a good homemade soup. It takes time to prepare but there is no substitute.

Soup is a great standby either on its own or as an accompaniment to a meal. Remember that soup can be filling, so choose a lighter soup as a starter or it could spoil the main course.

It is not necessary to boil soups for hours. It can be made and served immediately. Soup can be made in the morning and used in the evening but don't leave it boiling. Leave it to one side with a few knobs of butter on top so that a skin won't form and reheat it later by putting a little stock into a fresh saucepan and then adding the soup. This way it won't burn. It will also thin the soup which will have thickened a little when left lying.

The base of a good soup is the stock. The Chinese always use chicken stock in all their cooking because it is so delicate and contains very little grease. Sometimes you'll notice that it will jellify. Well that's good, as it means that there is plenty of nourishment in it. I like it as a base for a vegetable soup, which can be quite bland on its own. The following recipes are for four servings.

CHICKEN STOCK The only way to make a good chicken stock is to put the carcase of the chicken into a pot of cold water and bring it to the boil. The cold water heating up draws the goodness from the bones, whereas to douse it in boiling water would seal it in. Put a bouquet of vegetables – a chopped onion, a stick of celery, half a red and half a green pepper with a sprig of fennel – in the pot with the carcase. By the time all the water has come to the boil you have a good rich stock.

BROWN STOCK This is made with marrow bones bought quite cheaply from the butcher – if you are charged at all.

Trim all fat off the bones and put them on a tray in a very hot oven until brown and crisp. Then put them in a large pot and pour cold water over them. Add the bouquet of vegetables as for chicken stock and bring to the boil to make the stock.

1 pint (600ml) chicken stock
1 stick celery
½ onion
1 red pepper
1 green pepper
a sprig of fennel
salt and pepper
a good nob of butter
a little flour

Make sure you have a good chicken stock, because if the stock is not good the soup will be a disappointment.

Shred the vegetables finely as the pan is heating. When it is really hot add a good knob of butter and immediately afterwards put in the vegetables. The butter should not be allowed to clarify. Sauté the vegetables for a few minutes and season with salt and pepper as desired.

Using a wooden spoon blend in the flour with the vegetables. You only need enough to dust them. Sprinkle the flour and keep stirring in a figure-of-eight. You'll know they are cooked when they all congregate together in the middle of the pan. Slowly add the heated stock, a ladle at a time. If you add too much too fast you'll break the consistency of the roux. Taste it and serve.

POTATO SOUP

Dice the potatoes and brown in butter on the pan. (If you prefer you can boil the potatoes and use the stock, but I find it a bit bland and I think chicken stock gives the soup a better flavour.)

Remove the cooked potatoes and make a basic roux by sautéing the onion, celery and garlic – all finely chopped – on the pan and dusting with flour. Break down the consistency with heated chicken stock. Simmer for ten minutes. To serve, heat the diced potatoes in a little cream. Put some into each bowl and pour the strained stock over them.

4 potatoes
a little butter
a little flour
½ onion
2 sticks of celery
1 clove of garlic
1½ pints (850ml) chicken stock
a little cream

NOODLE SOUP

This soup goes down well at any time of the year. Light and nourishing, it is also a great favourite with children.

Cook the noodles in boiling water, giving them a stir to keep them apart. Chop the vegetables finely and sauté them on the pan. When all this is ready, strain the noodles and add them with the vegetables to the preheated chicken stock. Noodle soup does not need any thickening.

1 cup noodles
1 pint (600ml) chicken stock
1 stick of celery
1 carrot
½ onion

TOMATO SOUP

1 lb (450g) tomatoes
a little butter
a little flour
½ onion
2 sticks of celery
1 clove of garlic
1 tablespoon tomato ketchup
½ pint (300ml) chicken stock
a little malt vinegar
a little white sugar

Concasse the tomatoes – that is blanch them in boiling water, skin and chop them.

Sauté the onion, garlic and finely chopped celery. Add the tomatoes and a good spoon of tomato ketchup for colour with a little malt vinegar and sugar. Now dust with flour to bind, and break down the consistency with heated stock. Strain and serve.

MINESTRONE SOUP

½ onion
1 clove of garlic
2 rashers of streaky bacon
a little butter
a little flour
2 carrots
1 stick of celery
½ green pepper
½ red pepper
2 tomatoes
1½ pints (850ml) chicken stock
1 tablespoon tomato ketchup
1 oz (25g) cooked spaghetti
a little parmesan to sprinkle on top

Sauté the onion, garlic and bacon, all finely chopped, on a hot pan to bring out the flavour, using a little oil or butter. (If you use butter don't allow it to clarify.) Now add the rest of the vegetables, also finely chopped, and a knob of butter. Add a little flour to bind the vegetables and stir in a figure-of-eight until they congregate in the middle of the saucepan, which is an indication that you have the right consistency.

Now add the heated stock very gradually, stirring all the time to avoid lumps. This soup should not be boiled for ever as people seem to think. The vegetables in minestrone should be just cooked so that you can still taste them individually. The soup is right when the ladle is masked with a thin film.

Now add the cooked spaghetti, chopped small, and colour the minestrone with concassed tomatoes (see page 72). I don't use tinned tomatoes as they are too limp. Add a little tomato ketchup for extra colour – this has a richer colour and a milder flavour than tomato paste, which I find bitter.

Serve with parmesan cheese. This is good as a lunch with fresh rolls or garlic bread.

SOUPE À L'OIGNON (FRENCH ONION SOUP)

Cut the onions in half rings. Sauté them in the butter and a little oil until glassy. Gently add the flour stirring all the time in a figure-of-eight. When the onions seem to congregate in the centre it's right.

To avoid lumps make sure the stock is hot. Gradually add it to the roux, breaking down the consistency. Simmer and give it the ladle test – it's ready when the soup masks the spoon. Taste and adjust the seasoning.

You can serve this in individual dishes if you wish or in one large casserole. Toast slices of bread on both sides and remove crusts. Layer the bottom of the casserole with the cut slices and pour over the soup. When the bread rises to the top, sprinkle it with a good layer of parmesan and Gruyère and place in a hot oven until brown. Alternatively you can put it under the grill for a few minutes.

4 big onions
2 oz (50g) butter
a little oil
1 tablespoon flour
3 pints (1.75 litres) brown stock
5 slices bread
grated parmesan and Gruyère

BROWN ONION SOUP

This is a simpler onion soup, without the bread and cheese. Otherwise use the same ingredients as for the French onion soup, breaking down the consistency of the roux with beef or oxtail stock.

PRAWN CHOWDER

6–8 oz (175–225g) prawns or shrimps
1 pint (600ml) water
1 onion
2 sticks of celery
1 clove of garlic
1 rasher of bacon
1 red pepper
2 potatoes
a little flour
a little butter
parsley to garnish

The finest fish stock in the world is the liquid in which fresh prawns or shrimps have been cooked. Don't forget the golden rule – always use cold water first and then bring it to the boil. Save the stock. Make sure it doesn't continue to boil or it will make the soup bitter.

Sauté off some finely chopped onion, celery, garlic, strips of bacon and a red pepper. Separately blanch the diced potatoes in a little of the prawn stock.

Gently add a touch of flour to the vegetables in the pan to make a roux, stirring in a figure-of-eight. Gradually add the remainder of the stock. Before serving add the diced spuds and the prawns and sprinkle the soup with chopped parsley.

SEAFOOD CHOWDER

4 oz (100g) prawns
4 scallops
2 oysters
1 pint (600ml) water
1 onion
1 clove of garlic
2 sticks of celery
a little butter
a little flour

This soup is made with a velouté or fish stock in the same way as prawn chowder.

Make a stock by poaching the prawns, scallops and oysters, remembering not to boil it or it will be bitter. Remove the seafood. Then sauté the vegetables and make a roux with the butter and flour. Add the stock and let the soup simmer for five to ten minutes. Give it the ladle test – if the soup coats the ladle it has reached the right consistency.

Finally toss the seafood on a hot pan in a little butter to bring out the flavour before adding them to the pot.

SAUCES

WHITE SAUCE

1 oz (25g) flour
1 oz (25g) butter or margarine
½ pint (300ml) milk or stock
seasoning

A well-made sauce adds to any dish and the most common of all sauces is the basic white sauce. Usually made with flour, butter and milk, it can be poured over vegetables, fish, white meats etc or can be used as the basis of many other savoury sauces. Fish stock or chicken stock can be used instead of the milk.

The basis of the sauce is the roux, which is a blend of flour and butter. Where you want a thicker sauce add extra flour and for a thinner or a pouring sauce use more liquid.

To make the roux, melt the butter over a gentle heat, add the flour and cook for a minute or two. You'll see it begin to bubble.

Meanwhile have the liquid simmering – this will stop the sauce from going lumpy – and add it slowly to the roux. Keep stirring in a figure-of-eight to a creamy consistency. Bring the sauce to the boil and keep stirring as it thickens.

Season as desired.

PIQUANT SAUCE

½ onion
2 sticks of celery
1 clove of garlic
1 oz (25g) flour
1 oz (25g) butter or margarine
½ pint (300ml) beef stock

Brown off the onion, celery and garlic in a little butter and add the flour sparingly to make a roux. Strain on stock gradually until you have a creamy lump-free consistency.

DEVILLED SAUCE

This is just piquant sauce with a dash of cayenne or tabasco, depending on how hot you like it.

BEETROOT AND EGGWHITE SAUCE

1 cooked beetroot
whites of 2 hard-boiled eggs
1 cup piquant sauce

A variation on the standard piquant sauce, perfect served on the side with lamb cutlets. Mix chopped ingredients into sauce.

SWEET AND SOUR SAUCE

½ cup brown malt vinegar
½ cup tomato ketchup
½ cup pineapple juice

Mix the ingredients and heat gently. Do not boil – simmer. This is a transparent sauce, so no thickener is required.

THOUSAND ISLAND DRESSING

Just mix the liquid ingredients and add the finally chopped anchovies, celery, pepper, garlic and parsley, throw in a few capers – and there you have it.

1 carton of cream; a dash of brandy; a little tomato ketchup; a dash of tabasco; an anchovoy or two; 1 stick of celery; a small amount of red and green pepper; 1 clove of garlic; a little parsley; a few capers

HOMEMADE MAYONNAISE

This method is foolproof and does not have to be refrigerated – a sealed jar will do. Don't worry, it will never go bad as the oil and vinegar preserve the eggs.

Cream the eggs, mustard, sugar and pepper and salt and vinegar to a stiff consistency. Add the oil very slowly, running almost in a thread, to break down the consistency.

2 egg yolks; a little mustard; 3 tablespoons oil; 1 tablespoons vinegar; a little sugar; pepper and salt

TARTARE SAUCE

Simply add some Piccalilli for that sweet and sour flavour, finely chopped capers, onion and parsley to homemade mayonnaise.

MAYONNAISE MOUSSEUSE

Half mayonnaise, half whipped cream.

SPANISH MAYONNAISE

Mayonnaise with finely chopped garlic, a little cream and some very finely chopped cooked ham through it.

CUMBERLAND SAUCE

Spicy, nice with cold meats. Mix the ingredients.

1 cup redcurrant jelly; a little mustard; a dash of lemon juice; a dash of orange juice; a dash of Worcester sauce; a pinch of salt; a pinch of cayenne; a little sugar

BEARNAISE SAUCE

4 tablespoons tarragon
vinegar
chives or shallots
2 egg yolks
3 oz (75g) butter
variation
a small carton of cream
chopped parsley

This is the most difficult sauce in the culinary art to make. Some people use a double saucepan. It takes ages, but it's better than putting the pan directly on top of the stove.

The basis of the sauce is a reduction of tarragon vinegar and chives or shallots finely chopped. There should be enough vinegar to cover the circumference of the pan. Put this in the top of the double boiler if you are using one.

In the meantime, separate the egg yolks and pour a little water over them, enough to cover the yolk. The idea of the water is to give the eggs enough time to reach the consistency – otherwise they will scramble.

Clarify some butter on the side of the stove. The fat will rise and the sediment will sink.

Then add the eggs to the pan with the reduction in it, and stir in a figure-of-eight to a creamy consistency.

Remove the pan from the heat and add the clarified butter very slowly, making sure that no sediment goes in.

Alternatively, you can use unsweetened whipped cream and chopped parsley instead of butter.

HOLLANDAISE SAUCE

4 oz (100g) butter
3 egg yolks
2 teaspoons lemon juice
salt

Another slow sauce, and the double boiler – or a bowl in a pan of hot water – is a must for this. The water should be hot but not boiling in the double boiler, otherwise the sauce will thicken too quickly.

Melt the butter first in the top of the double saucepan and then add the egg yolks which have been beaten lightly with the lemon juice and salt. Keep stirring in a figure-of-eight all the time until the sauce is smooth and creamy.

VINAIGRETTE DRESSING (FRENCH DRESSING)

3 parts oil
1 part vinegar
1 teaspoon dry mustard
1 clove of garlic
seasoning
¼ teaspoon sugar (optional)

Crush the garlic and mix ingredients thoroughly, adding a little sugar if you find the dressing too sharp.

SOUR CREAM

Unsweetened tinned milk with a dash of lemon juice makes excellent sour cream.

CHOCOLATE SAUCE

Simply use melted cooking chocolate. For a de luxe finish add a nip of Cointreau.

JUBILEE SAUCE

6 oz (175g) butter
6 oz (175g) sugar
1 orange
1 lemon

This dessert sauce is useful for several dishes. It's good as a sauce with custard, fresh fruits, banana, pineapple, apple, strawberry and even peaches. Use it with pancakes too.

Squeeze the juice from the orange and lemon and save the skins. Have the pan really hot and rub the skins of the orange and lemon around the pan until it goes brown. Throw out the skins.

Now the pan has the flavour of the fruits. Add the butter now and then the sugar. Next carmelise the butter and sugar. Use a fork to blend them together, and take a little time so that they go a nice golden brown like toffee. Don't worry if the mixture looks lumpy.

Add just a little drop of lemon and orange juice to break down the carmel, then slowly add the rest of the juice.

SALADS

Salads, I am glad to say, have come into their own in Ireland over the past few years and we are slowly but surely getting away from the traditional limp lettuce leaves with sliced egg and tomato. Salads should be crisp, crunchy and a colourful combination of fresh flavours.

Most vegetables and fruits combine well together. As well as greens like cabbage, lettuce and chicory, grated raw vegetables, nuts, seeds, cooked beans and rice are popular bases for salads.

Like soup, salads are good as starters. A crisp green salad can also be served between courses to cleanse the palate. Salads can be fortified with strips of cooked meat if necessary and served as a main course.

Generally salads should be tossed just before serving. However, root vegetables benefit if tossed in mayonnaise or French dressing a few hours before serving.

Remember that most of the nutrition in fruit and vegetables lies just beneath the skin. Scrub rather than scrape carrots and chop apples for salads without peeling them.

AVOCADO TOMATO SALAD BOWL

Pour the oil and half the lemon juice over the tomatoes cut into eighths and chill. Cut the avocado lengthwise, remove the stone, peel and cut into slices. Toss with the shredded greens and tomatoes. Season.

4 tablespoons olive or salad oil
4 tablespoons lemon juice
3 tomatoes
1 avocado
a small bunch watercress
½ teaspoon celery salt
1 clove of garlic
½ head lettuce
½ head chicory

CEASAR SALAD

Rub the garlic around the salad bowl. Put the shredded lettuce into the bowl, add the egg yolk, anchovies and parmesan and mix together with two wooden spoons. This is a lovely combination served with the croutons.

1 clove of garlic
a head of lettuce
1 egg yolk
a few anchovies
a little parmesan cheese
a few croutons

SUMMER HERB SALAD

Combine all the ingredients and add French dressing.

mustard greens
spinach
marjoram
lettuce leaves
rosemary
summer savory
tarragon
French dressing

TOMATO AND ONION RINGS

I like this as a starter as well as a side dish. Choose firm medium sized tomatoes, and slice evenly. Slice the onion rings finely. Marinate in French dressing, onions on the bottom of the bowl, before serving. Toss carefully.

1 small onion
3 tomatoes
French dressing

EGG MAYONNAISE

Easy and staple food. Good for buffets and as a starter. One egg per person is plenty. Hard-boil the eggs and halve them. Place the cut side down on a bed of lettuce and coat with homemade mayonnaise. Sprinkle with paprika. Garnish with anchovies if you like.

CUCUMBER SALAD

Peel the cucumber if the skin is very tough. Slice it finely and sprinkle with salt. Press between two plates and drain after twenty minutes. Some people say this treatment makes the cucumber more digestible. It tastes good, and is excellent in sandwiches.

TUNA SALAD

To equal amounts of tuna fish – tinned will do – and French beans add some tomato wedges and cucumber slices, a few olives and French dressing and there you have it. Delicious with toasted brown bread.

PASTA SALAD

Any small pasta is ideal. Cook for about fifteen minutes making sure there is still a little 'bone' left. Drain and rinse in cold water. Toss in a bowl with French dressing and add chopped red and green peppers, black olives and tomato quarters.

GREEN SALADS

Vary the lettuce leaves with finely shredded cabbage, spinach, Chinese leaves, chicory or curly endive.
   Toss in French dressing until it glistens.

BEETROOT SALAD

Fresh small whole cooked beetroots submerged in malt vinegar before serving.

COLESLAW

Possibly the most popular of all side dishes – finely shredded carrots, cabbage and a little onion tossed in mayonnaise.
   Vary this by using French dressing occasionally.

POTATO SALAD When done properly, this is lovely. The potatoes should be cooked to the point where there is still some 'bone' in them. Then cut them into even squares and add some finely chopped onion, parsley, pepper and salt and a touch only of mayonnaise – sour cream is even nicer.

EGG AND ENDIVE SALAD Lightly poach an egg and drop it on top of a bowl of crisp garlicky endives and stir it through.

SALAD AS A MAIN COURSE Diced chicken, ham, lamb or pork added to a salad fortifies a dish. Add to chopped celery, nuts, sweet apples (unpeeled) which have been soaked in lemon juice to avoid browning – all the nutrition you need. Toss in mayonnaise.

As you can see salads can be made up from any combination. Try green peppers and oranges together tossed in French dressing. It looks good as well. Cooked rice with red and green peppers, mushrooms, apples and even pineapple is delicious and refreshing.

SNACKS & SAVOURIES

Made from oysters rolled in bacon. Skewer with a wooden cocktail stick and bake on a tray in the oven.

ANGELS ON HORSEBACK

Cheddar is usually the best cheese for cooking. Red or white will do. Dust some cheese strips in flour very lightly before dipping them into a light batter (see page 82). The flour will make the batter cling. Drain off any excess. Drop into very hot oil, cook until golden brown and drain on greaseproof paper before serving with a touch of cayenne pepper. Delicate as well as delicious.

CHEESE FRITTERS

Roasted chicken legs are a great favourite. The meat maintains its moistness more than beef or any other meat. Good for parties and picnics. They can be deep fried plain or dipped in egg wash and breadcrumbs, or baked in their own juices. Try sprinkling with lemon juice for a change.

CHICKEN LEGS

Mince the chicken and season to taste. Shape as for croquette potatoes (see page 68), dust in flour, dip in egg wash, coat with breadcrumbs and deep fry. Then put them on greaseproof paper to keep them crispy and dry.

CHICKEN NUGGETS

These are essential for the kitchen hawk. You've met him before, especially at house weddings and parties. Despite the fact that he's eaten exactly the same as everybody else, he'll be starving – so be prepared.
   Butter the bread on both sides and toast under the grill. Then layer on the crispy bread, hard-fried egg, slices of tomato, coleslaw, a touch of mayonnaise and some homemade game chips – or shop crisps will do – just keep going, layer after layer until he begs for mercy.

CLUB SANDWICHES

Sautéed chicken livers rolled in streaky bacon devilled with Worcester sauce and baked in the oven. These look good speared with wooden sticks as kebabs.

DEVILS ON HORSEBACK

DUBLIN TOAST　This makes a popular change from cheese. It's a Welsh rarebit made with grated Cheddar and the yoke of an egg, some dried Colman's mustard, a nip of Worcester sauce and an eggcup of Guinness, which gives it all a wonderful flavour. If you find it is inclined to be runny simply add more grated cheese. Serve on toast – the best hint I can give is to butter the bread on both sides – it will taste really succulent and the combination looks great.

EGGS HOLLANDAISE　Scrambled eggs mixed with flaked smooked haddock and served on a round of toast.

FRENCH TOAST　Simple to make this classic. Dip a slice of bread with the crusts removed into beaten egg and milk and fry on a hot pan in some oil until golden brown. Sprinkle cinnamon over the toast before serving, making sure to place the toast on kitchen paper to blot off the excess oil first.

GARLIC BREAD　Make garlic butter by creaming a few crushed cloves of garlic in an ounce or two of butter. Break a French stick into segments, slice them lengthwise and butter with garlic butter. Leave in a hot oven until the crust is crispy.

HERRING ROE ON TOAST　Cook the roe on the pan and place under the grill on toast having first sprinkled it with paprika. A good starter.

IVANHOE　Finely pounded smoked haddock minced with a little thin white sauce (page 95) and some whipped cream and cayenne pepper. Serve on buttered toast and decorate with a flat field mushroom.

PIGS' TROTTERS　A delicacy. Ask the butcher to cut them in half through the toes. Clean and boil to a jelly with mustard added to the water. Remove the trotters from the pot and allow to get cold. Then simply breadcrumb them and sprinkle a pinch of mustard on top and place in the oven until golden brown.

Wrap the pineapple pieces in bacon and cook in the oven. A nice combination of flavours.

PINEAPPLE AND BACON

You can never go wrong with a nice sandwich. Ribbon sandwiches consist of up to ten different ingredients like chicken, turkey, smoked salmon, beef, tomatoes, lettuce and plenty of dressing to keep it moist, between several layers of bread. The more colourful the layers the better. The sandwich is pressed and served in slices. Substantial and looks wonderful.

SANDWICHES

Children will love them cold if they are nice and crispy. Don't forget to blanch the sausages in boiling water first – the skin stretches and they won't burst – before cooking them in the oven for perfect results. Wrap them in lettuce leaves if you are serving them on a picnic.

SAUSAGES

Hard-boil the eggs. Run under the cold tap until cool. Roll them under your hand and they will shell easily.

Make a mixture of sausage meat and homemade breadcrumbs (one-third crumbs to two-third sausage meat). Dust the eggs in flour and roll them in the mixture. Knead gently with your hands until you have the eggs back to their oval shape.

Deep fry in a medium hot oil. If you are worried whether the sausage meat is cooked properly, place them in the oven for five minutes to finish them off.

SCOTCH EGGS

This is simply scrambled egg on a round of toast. Decorate with anchovy fillets in an X with a rolled anchovy in the centre, topped with capers.

SCOTCH WOODCOCK

COURGETTES WITH CARROTS AND FRESH MINT

This is a suitable dish on its own or with rice for supper or lunch.

Judge the size of the vegetables and adjust the quantities, as needed. Cut the carrots into quarter-inch rounds. Heat the saucepan. Use about two tablespoons of butter and add the sliced carrots. Cook for about five minutes until they are half-cooked. Then add the courgettes and a little Madeira. Cook for a further five minutes until the vegetables are crispy and tender.

Sprinkle with finely chopped mint and serve.

2–3 courgettes
3–4 carrots
a little butter or margarine
a drop of Madeira
a few mint leaves

RICE WITH ALMONDS AND RAISINS
good as a lunch or supper

Heat a saucepan on the stove slowly, until it is very hot. Add the butter, finely chopped onion, raisins, almonds and rice. Then pour in the stock, stirring the rice through it so that the other ingredients are not stuck to the bottom of the saucepan.

Cook with the lid on until all the liquid is absorbed – about twenty minutes.

1 tablespoon butter
2 cups rice
¼ cup blanched almonds
2 teaspoons raisins
½ onion
1½ cups chicken stock

DISH FOR 4

½ lb (225g) thin noodles
4 tomatoes
1 clove of garlic
2 tablespoons butter
parmesan cheese

Drop the noodles into boiling water and cook until tender. Stir with a wooden spoon to prevent them sticking together. Drain the cooked noodles and wash under the cold tap.

Heat a saucepan, add two tablespoonfuls of hard butter with a small clove of finely chopped garlic. Then add the noodles. Concasse the tomatoes (see page 82) and stir the noodles gently before adding the tomato concasse.

Serve with parmesan cheese on the side.

NOODLES WITH FRESH TOMATOES
vegetarian supper or lunch

DISH FOR 4

¾ lb (350g) spaghetti
2 cloves of garlic
2 rashers of bacon
3 onions
4 oz (100g) mushrooms
6 tomatoes

Quick and good for lunches or suppers. Spaghetti is a good traveller and a handy dish to take to weekend cottages or even on picnics. It is reheated on a hot pan with a knob of butter.

Cook the spaghetti — it should be al dente and have a little bone in it still.

A simple Neapolitan sauce is made up by sautéeing in oil the chopped garlic, bacon, onions and finally the mushrooms, adding the concassed tomatoes at the end. Serve in a separate dish on the side.

Green salad (see page 13) and garlic bread (see page 104) make a meal of this.

SPAGHETTI NEAPOLITANA
with a green salad and garlic bread

QUICHE LORRAINE
served hot or cold

A very popular bacon and egg flan, but you can use mushrooms, tomatoes and onions too if you like. Quiche is ideal for suppers and lunches and is good served with side salads for a cold meal.

Line a ring or baking tray with the pastry. Cover it with lightly sautéed strips of bacon and the grated cheese.

Beat the eggs with the cream and pour over the filling.

Bake in a moderate oven (gas mark 5–6; 375°F; 190°C) for half an hour.

6 oz (175g) unsweetened shortcrust pastry
3 eggs
a carton of cream
3 oz (75g) Gruyère or Cheddar cheese
2–3 rashers of bacon

HINTS

Try to use real plates for picnics and barbecues. Paper plates absorb the goodness and the food ends up tasting like paper. There is no substitute for the real thing. **AL FRESCO EATING**

Meat transports well wrapped in greaseproof paper. Tinfoil is not good. If you wrap meat in tinfoil you create condensation.

Put peeled and chopped apples in a bowl of water with a little salt added to keep them from growing brown. **APPLES**

Cover the bowl of batter with a clean kitchen cloth and allow it to stand. This gives the batter a chance to ferment. **BATTER**

Avoid using little foil packs of butter. They are awkward to handle. A plain slab of butter garnished with parsley looks better too. **BUTTER**

A lot of people like to use butter in cooking, and they are not very successful because they allow the butter to clarify before they start to cook. The way to avoid this is to put your butter on the hot pan and immediately afterwards add your ingredients, which will cool the pan and prevent the butter from clarifying.

Before carving your meat, always leave it to set, even if only for a few minutes. It will be easier to carve. **CARVING**

Cheddar cheese is best for most recipes. **CHEESE**

Never wrap cheese in plastic – allow it to breathe.

Use a single block of wood – anything else is a health hazard. Clean your chopping board with lemon juice or oil if you use it for different types of food – otherwise keep separate boards for meat and for vegetables. **CHOPPING BOARDS**

I recommend a skillet or very heavy frying pan to cook these. Have it very hot. Seal the meat, drain off the excess fat and finish off in the oven. Lamb doesn't take long but pork should be well done. **CHOPS**

111

For lamb make a little sauce with a little rosemary, garlic, onion in a knob of butter. Then add a drop of red wine and cream. Likewise with steak, using the meat residue and some finely chopped spring onion, a little garlic and mushroom. Sauté in the butter add a drop of cream or wine and you have a beautiful sauce, with the goodness of the meat juices.

CROQUETTES Always put fish or chicken croquettes which have been dipped in egg and breadcrumbs into very hot deep fat. This way the breadcrumbs won't soak up the oil.

Remember it's the heat of your hand which binds the croquettes, so don't use lots of flour.

EGGS To avoid eggs sticking to the bottom of the pot when poaching add a drop of lemon juice or vinegar.

Save the water eggs have been poached in to wash albumen egg stains off silver spoons.

Hard-boiled eggs should not be cooked for longer than nine minutes to avoid a black rim around the yolk. Cool under the cold tap and shell.

FONDUE You must have hot drinks with a cheese fondue, otherwise the cheese will coat the roof of your mouth.

FRENCH DRESSING If you find it is too strong, break a lightly boiled egg over the mixture before serving. This tones down the sharp flavours.

FRITTERS Always drain off excess batter before putting fritters in the hot oil. Use fresh fruit only — never tinned.

FRYING Use a tongs rather than a fork when turning meat, as a fork punctures the flesh and releases the juices.

GARLIC

To stop garlic sticking to your knife sprinkle it with salt before chopping.

KIDNEYS

Always blanch before cooking. If a kidney bobs to the top of the water it's not fresh.

When cooking steak and kidney pie always cook the kidney separately.

KITCHEN SAFETY

There are a few commonsense rules that go with good cooking.

You should never leave the kitchen if you have something on the stove.

The kitchen should be designed so that you could put your hand on whatever you need even if the lights were to go out.

You should never take a pot off the stove without a dry cloth in your hand. A damp cloth could create steam and give a nasty burn.

KNIVES

You should use good quality kitchen knives. Stainless steel ones won't go black. Keep separate knives for vegetables and for meat and don't use them for odd-jobs like snipping the string on parcels.

LIVER

This is best cooked fast and it's more digestible when underdone.

MANGOES

Peeling a mango is not as easy as it looks. Slice each side. Criss-cross the mango flesh. Then hold the fruit at each end and bend until the flesh comes up through the skin and you can eat it in comfort.

MERINGUES

Before you put them in the oven 'prove' them first. The best place is the airing cupboard or somewhere in the kitchen where there is a constant warm (not hot) temperature.

MINCED MEAT

Ordinary mince has a very high fat content, so choose round steak and ask the butcher to mince it for you. Make sure you ask him to clean out the mincer first.

MINT Sprinkle mint with sugar to stop it sticking to the knife when chopping.

ONIONS To prevent onions from bringing tears to your eyes or to prevent them repeating when eaten, soak them in some cold water with a teaspoonful of bicarbonate of soda to six onions. Leave them in the water for fifteen minutes before peeling.

OVEN COOKING You'll probably notice that with a lot of my dishes I start on the top of the stove and finish off in the oven. The reason for this is that it guarantees perfect cooking throughout.

For this method to work the oven must be good and hot to start.

OVEN GLOVES These are banned from my kitchen, especially those which are attached at the ends like handcuffs. Two dry clothes give more control over scalding pots.

OYSTERS Never wash oysters. It takes all the goodness and flavour out of them.

PANS You must have two pans, one for omelettes and one for everything else, otherwise the albumen in eggs sticks to the pan.

Use good quality pans – a black iron pan is fine. Don't wash it, but clean it with a damp cloth and a drop of oil – washing spoils the surface. A drop of lemon juice will remove odours like garlic or onion. To remove rust from an iron pan put a layer of rock salt into the pan and put it in a hot oven – wooden handle removed, of course – until it turns red.

Make sure the pan is hot before you cook anything in it. This goes for all receptacles. If you try to cook in a cold pan then you have have all sorts of difficulties. By the time the pan or pot heats you have drawn all the goodness out of your ingredients.

POTS Store these singly, not one inside the other, as this damages the surfaces, and even the slightest pin hole is a health hazard. I suggest a wall rack for storing lids – it is important that they should fit snugly so that they don't allow steam to escape in cooking.

PRESENTATION This is very important. People 'eat with their eyes'. Heat the plates. Remember hot food should be really hot. Rather than bringing the lot to the table and trying to keep it hot over a lamp it's better to bring in the dishes from the kitchen only as they are needed. Believe it or not badly cooked food served hot tastes better than good food that has been allowed to get cold.

Never put anything direct from the pan on to the plate you are eating from, first put in on one dish and transfer it. This will leave any excess oil or fat behind.

Sauces usually look better served on the side. This does not include dishes cooked in sauce of course.

Vegetables should also be served in separate dishes.

Give attention to detail – make sure there are no pips in lemon wedges and trim the white sinews so that the lemon will squeeze on to the food and not into your eye.

RASHERS Best cooked in the oven. The even heat gives a lovely crispy rasher.

RASPBERRIES These should never be washed as this takes all the flavour out of them. Simply cleanse them by shaking in a dry clean cloth.

SADDLE OF LAMB Always carve against the grain for a more even distribution of fat.

SAUCES When you have made fish or meat sauce, it is advisable to place a few knobs of butter on top of the sauce to prevent a skin forming.

Similarly when making a sweet or custard sauce sprinkle some sugar on top to prevent a skin.

SAUSAGES Blanch first in boiling water to stretch the skin and avoid bursting. Best cooked in the oven.

SCRAMBLED EGGS Don't add milk or water because it breaks down the consistency and turns the eggs green.

SOUP To heat soup put a little stock in the bottom of the pot first and then add the soup. This way it won't stick.

STEAK A rare steak needs a very hot pan, the hotter the better. Seal the steak on both sides. For medium and well-done steaks use the oven to ensure that they are quite cooked, rather than cremating them on the stove.

   Have the pan really hot. Use only a small drop of oil. Seal the steak on top of the cooker. Give it about five minutes, turn with a tongs, put it on a tray and bake in a hot oven for ten to fifteen minutes, seven to ten for a medium steak. All the goodness will be there in that tray. You can brown the steak under the grill for a minute if you like and then pour the juices and blood from the dish over the steak and serve.

STUFFING Stuffing for turkey, chicken etc to my mind should always be cooked separately. Then there won't be any worries about whether the bird is cooked throughout.

TOAST Butter the bread on both sides before toasting for a really succulent toast.

TURKEY Test for freshness and tenderness by pressing your finger on the breast bone. If it is spongy to the touch the turkey is tender. Do not use tinfoil in the cooking as this steams the bird. Do not tie the legs as this prevents the natural juices from being fully absorbed and you end up with that portion of the meat undercooked. Baste turkey regularly to avoid burning and when the socks are showing and the

116

parson's nose is pointy you can be sure it's done. The same applies to chicken.

To reheat turkey cover it with greaseproof paper and place in a medium oven with a knob of butter. Leave it until the paper turns brown. The result is a lovely juicy turkey as good as the first day it was cooked.

VEGETABLES

Soak in salt water. This kills all green fly and slugs.

You'll notice in all my recipes where vegetables and meat are involved, I always sauté the vegetables before adding the meat. The reason for this is that if you add the meat first it will release its juices which will make the vegetables soggy.

WINE

Vintage red wine should be opened beforehand to allow it to reach room temperature. White wine should be served chilled or not at all.

When cooking with wine don't add cold wine to food. Heat it gently first.

INDEX

119